CW00540125

Making it Work

Good practice with young carers and their families

Jenny Frank

This book belongs to:

Young Carers Service

First published in 2002

The Children's Society
Edward Rudolf House
Margery Street
London WC1X 0JL

The Princess Royal Trust for Carers
142 The Minories
London EC3N 1LB

A catalogue record of this book is available from the British Library.

ISBN 1 899783 46 6

Contents

Section 2: Putting it into Practice

Appendix: Annotated Bibliography

Acknowledgements

This Good Practice Guide represents what is understood about best practice at this point in time. It only exists because of the contributions made by young carers, their families, and professionals involved in working with them.

It is hoped that this guide will prove to be a useful starting point for good practice to evolve further across all agencies. Inter-agency and holistic approaches are vital if we are to meet the needs of young carers and their families effectively and appropriately.

Listening to them needs to be the starting point.

> *"Recognise that our family is probably the 'expert' on the situation and work towards what our family wants."*
> (Young carer quoted in The Children's Society, 2000)

The content of this guide is a direct result of a consultation process. Consultation with young carers took place directly during the Young Carers' Festivals held in 2000, 2001 and 2002, jointly organised by The Children's Society and South East Hampshire YMCA at Fairthorne Manor. An evaluation was also undertaken in 2002 to ask young carers and their families about what they felt worked well, and where they saw the gaps in services and support. Their views underpin the content of this guide.

In addition, The Children's Society has held a number of seminars for professionals who are involved in supporting young carers and their families. Topics included: issues for health professionals, schools, social workers, and the role of the voluntary organisations; assessments; and the specific needs of sibling carers. Issues for those caring for someone with mental ill health or involved in substance misuse were also discussed. Learning shared at these seminars has helped to inform this guide.

The guide also uses material from published research and a range of local practice materials, including consultations and evaluations. These materials include direct local consultation with children, young people and their families.

The Princess Royal Trust for Carers has assisted with provision of case studies and project materials, and many of the individual carers' centres have been involved throughout the consultation.

We would also like to acknowledge the support of The Balcombe Trust.

This publication would not have been possible without the tireless assistance of Alison Kendall; the invaluable editorial input of Jacqui Woods and Annabel Warburg; and the design and typesetting flair of Neil Adams.

Forewords

I would like to thank The Children's Society and Princess Royal Trust for Carers for producing this guide and giving me the opportunity to contribute some thoughts. We are committed to raising standards in education and improving the life chances for all our children. Therefore it is important that we understand the issues specific to young carers that might impede their access to a high quality education. Professionals must explore means of supporting the educational needs of these young people whilst acknowledging their caring responsibilities.

Research indicates that poor attendance at school and low educational achievement have an influence on social exclusion in later life, and young people with caring responsibilities may be particularly at risk. It is therefore important to ensure that schools are as supportive of young carers as they can be so that these young people have the best chance of fulfilling their potential.

Chapter 5 of this guide contains powerful messages from young carers as well as practical advice for teachers and other professionals. This will help to improve identification of this group and provision of appropriate support. I believe that this guide illustrates the value of a multi-agency approach to working with young carers and school communities to ensure that they are provided with a suitable education in all circumstances.

Stephen Twigg MP,
Parliamentary Under-Secretary of State for
Young People and Learning

This practice guidance is an important document. It has the potential to improve the lives of thousands of young carers and their families. Reading it, I am struck by a number of themes which come up time and again in our work with children.

First, there is the overriding need to listen to the children themselves. They have a right to be heard, and are often best placed to know what is right for them and their families. This is all the more important for young carers, who are often shouldering adult responsibilities.

Second, each young carer and each family needs to be approached as an individual. No two families are identical, so it is unlikely that identical solutions will be appropriate either.

Third, there is a need for more cohesive services for children and their families. Too often, it is they who have to fit themselves round the needs of organisations. This cannot be right. I am determined to see it change, so that children and families who need help experience a seamless service.

This practice guide clearly points the way to improve all of these issues. I am delighted to support it, and look forward to seeing the improvements it will help to drive forward.

Jacqui Smith MP,
Minister of State for Health

"The All Party Parliamentary Group for Children consistently supports the principle of listening to children on issues which affect them. The Group has held meetings with young carers who presented their concerns in a moving and powerful way. We are pleased that this is being taken up by cross-Government Departments."

Baroness Massey of Darwen,
Chairperson, All Party Parliamentary Group for Children

Position statements

The Children's Society

The Children's Society believes that:

> **"All children and young people are able to participate in their neighbourhoods and in the services which affect their lives; their thoughts and wishes should be taken into account and they should be empowered in making informed decisions about their lives."**

Listening to children and enabling them to have a voice is integral to all the activities of The Children's Society. In its work with young carers, the Society has always advocated considering a **whole-family approach** to meet the needs of the child, whilst enabling the child to be informed, consulted and supported (Frank, 1995). The Children's Society will continue to advocate for:

- improved practice and increased effective service provision for families;
- continued awareness-raising of needs;
- improved consultation with the whole family in order to:
  - better meet the needs of all family members,
  - reduce the impact of disability or illness on the child and family life,
  - support parenting needs;
- young carers' needs to be acknowledged, assessed and appropriate support offered;
- young carers to be informed, consulted and given choices about whether or not they wish to care and, if they do, how they wish to be identified and supported.

The Young Carers Initiative is funded by the Department of Health to develop a coherent focus for young carers, their families and those who work to support them, to promote common standards and to work towards realisation of equitable services. For more information, email young-carers-initiative@childrenssociety.org.uk

The Princess Royal Trust for Carers

The Princess Royal Trust
for Carers

The Princess Royal Trust for Carers (PRTC) recognises that a significant number of children and young people under the age of 18 take on practical and/or emotional caring responsibilities that would normally be expected of an adult. We also recognise that a child or young person living in a household where there is disability or long-term illness may be affected in a variety of different ways, regardless of whether she/he takes on caring responsibilities. The impact may continue into adulthood.

We believe that all such children and young people have a right to be supported in order to cope with their situation, and to have choices in determining what constitutes appropriate support. All such support should be provided within the context of support for the whole family. All such support should also be aware of issues surrounding child protection and should work within accepted procedures for child protection. We work to promote cross-agency approaches wherever possible. Whatever the approaches adopted, they should enable parents to fulfil their parenting role whilst minimising the impact of caring on children and young people.

The network of PRTC Carers' Centres supports young carers through both specialist projects and partnerships with other local service providers. They provide support services directly to young carers and seek to raise awareness of the needs and contribution of young carers within health, social care, education and other appropriate agencies. They also work to secure better services for the whole family.

Each PRTC Carers' Centre develops its support services for young carers according to locally agreed need and the resources available. They seek at all times to work within the legislative framework for young carers. Over time the Princess Royal Trust will develop a series of statements on specific policy issues relating to work with young carers. For more information, email info@carers.org

Section 1

Setting the Scene

Introduction

Over recent years, awareness of young carers' issues has been raised considerably by many organisations, including The Children's Society, The Princess Royal Trust for Carers, The Young Carers Research Group at Loughborough University, Barnardo's, NCH, Crossroads for Carers and Carers UK. This has resulted in the development of projects and services working to support young carers and their families across the United Kingdom.

A wealth of good practice and learning relating to work with young carers and their families has now evolved. This, in turn, has led to a range of support for some of the many children in caring roles. However, there is no equity of provision for either the children or the person in need of care. Consequently, support is good in some areas, but more sparse in others. For many authorities, the will to support these families exists, but the resources do not. Undoubtedly, this uneven spread means that a significant number of children and families remain in need.

Who is this practice guide for?

The needs of young carers and their families are a multi-agency responsibility that crosses both adults' and children and families' services. This practice guide is therefore aimed at **all** agencies that have contact with young carers and the people for whom they care. It brings together much of the thinking and experience behind the good practice developed so far and will provide a useful starting point for those new to this area of work and serve as a development resource for the more experienced.

There are now many publications on the support of young carers, so what makes this practice guide any different?

- It draws directly on the views of young carers and their families.
- It promotes an inter-agency and holistic approach.
- It offers the reader realistic, practical suggestions for the development of support services for young carers and their families.
- It presents current legislation and policy guidelines clearly, relating them to recommendations for practical work.
- It contains a detailed and fully annotated bibliography.

In short, this guide is a useful tool for all practitioners and those involved in the planning of services.

CHAPTER 1
Context, needs and issues

Background

Over the past ten years, a wide range of research has been undertaken into the needs of young carers and the impact that inappropriate levels of caring has on their own well-being and development. There have been a number of consistent findings. The research has shown that children who are living in a family where there is physical or mental illness, disability, or alcohol or substance misuse, may be caring in a number of different ways. Many are involved in giving what may be considered inappropriate levels of care for a child to undertake. They might be offering practical assistance around the home, undertaking physical care such as lifting, or personal care such as dressing, washing and toileting. They may assist with therapy or giving medication. Many also undertake care and responsibility for younger siblings.

Research has also highlighted the fact that caring has a high emotional element for children. Many have described the worry and anxiety that they experience when someone who is close to them is ill or disabled. Those who do not give any practical or physical care may still be giving emotional support, and experiencing a range of emotions, anxieties and stress.

Caring for a relative at home is not a recent phenomenon. However, the impact of caring in a climate where the extended family unit is no longer commonplace and where health and social services are both understaffed and under-resourced, can be far reaching – especially when the carer is under 18.

> "Identifying young people with caring responsibilities for a relative at home is difficult – they may not have the language, confidence or self-awareness to relay the physical and/or emotional impact of living with a relative who requires care, let alone identify themselves as having caring responsibilities."
>
> (Baker, PRTC, 2002)

Research and evidence from practice has also shown that, for a range of reasons, young carers are often hidden and their needs and those of the person for whom they are caring are only identified when there is a crisis. Even then, the extent of their caring role and the impact that it has on their own development, may not be recognised quickly or fully assessed.

> *"It was when I happened to fall asleep in a class that they found out my Mum was ill. It's not the sort of thing that comes up... I didn't used to talk to anyone. I suppose that was my*

own fault in a way, but then I didn't know anyone was interested."

(Young carer quoted in Clark, 1996)

This chapter considers what is meant by the term 'young carer' – how they are defined in terms of legislation but also how they define themselves. It goes on to discuss in more detail who young carers are – how many there may be, the kinds of caring they do, and how they may have come to assume this role. In particular, this chapter focuses on the effects that caring may have on the children and young people, drawing on case studies and quotes from young carers themselves. The final section looks at some of the current support systems and services that are in place for young carers and their families.

MAKING IT WORK

Recognise that young carers may be hidden and consider pro-active practice that will enable families to feel able to ask for support.

Defining a young carer

Several definitions of a 'young carer' exist in current legislation and guidance. In 1995, the Social Services Inspectorate defined a young carer as:

"A child or young person (under age 18) who is carrying out significant caring tasks and assuming a level of responsibility for another person, which would usually be taken by an adult."

(Department of Health, 1995, Chief Inspector letter C1 (95)12)

The Carers' (Recognition and Services) Act 1995 uses the definition:

"Children and young people (under 18) who provide or intend to provide a substantial amount of care on a regular basis."

A detailed discussion of the existing legislation used to define young carers can be found in Baker (PRTC, 2002). It concludes that "current legislation, even the most recent, does little to stop or support children caring for a relative at home".

In 1998, the Carers National Association (now Carers UK) defined a young carer as:

"anyone under the age of 18 *whose life is in some way restricted* because of the need to take responsibility for the care of someone who is ill, has a disability, is experiencing mental distress, or is affected by substance misuse."

This last definition highlights the importance of taking into account not only the extent and nature of caring but also the actual or potential impact it has on the young carer.

MAKING IT WORK

It is important to take into account not only the extent and nature of caring, but also the actual or potential impact it has on the child.

"A young carer is someone of 16 years of age or younger, who because of a parent's disability undertakes essential and perhaps non-essential caring tasks (personal care, housework, fetching and carrying) over and above what

would normally be expected of their peer group. They may also be undertaking this role willingly, or through necessity because the disabled parent is not receiving this assistance from social services, or from a responsible adult. By 'disabled parent' I also include a parent with a drug or alcohol addiction, or long-term illness."

(Disabled parent)

"What is a young carer? Well we could say that within a family we all care for each other and are involved in helping and assisting each other every day. In a family where there is a disabled member, then often the 'assisting and helping tasks' are somewhat different to that in a family where there isn't disability. It is when a young person/child has to take on some or all responsibility for these tasks because there isn't another adult partner to do so that this youngster becomes defined as the 'young carer'. I would say that this is especially true when the tasks involved means the child becomes excluded from the 'normal' activities and somewhat carefree life of a child."

(Disabled parent)

There is a continuum of caring onto which all children fit somewhere. The question is at what point, in what circumstances and by whom should these children be classed as 'young carers'? It is important to differentiate between a 'normal' level of 'caring' within a family and a level of inappropriate physical or emotional caring that affects a child's own personal, social and educational development. Moreover, some children see themselves as young carers, while others do not. It is important to listen to their points of view about definition and perception.

When asked, children tend to describe their situations in terms of feelings and tasks rather that attempt a definition of 'young carer'.

MAKING IT WORK

Recognise that there are different perspectives on the definition of a young carer. It is important to listen to the young people's points of view.

"We are part of a family and have feelings that need to be recognised. We have all sorts of feelings. We can feel protective, angry, upset, hurt, worried, anxious and uncertain."

(Young carer quoted in The Children's Society, 2000)

"Halfway through the year I started to let myself go. I could no longer be strong...instead I became a feeble little girl. Mum got worse which meant more responsibility. I was cooking dinner, doing five to six pieces of homework a night and looking after my sister. That was it, I had a nervous breakdown and became very withdrawn to society, never went out much anyway. But I was constantly crying."

(Sam, aged 15, quoted in Baker, PRTC, 2002)

Young carers also need to be differentiated from those children and young people who share some of their circumstances but cannot be defined as young carers themselves because they are not caring for someone who has an illness or disability. For example:

- children who 'baby-sit' siblings in families where parents are voluntarily absenting their parenting responsibilities (to go to work, etc);
- teenage mothers.

It is also important to remember that **not** every child whose parent/brother/sister is ill or disabled is necessarily a young carer.

MAKING IT WORK

Remember – not every child whose parent/ sibling is ill or disabled is necessarily a young carer.

The following is the definition of young carers given in *The Blackwell Encyclopaedia of Social Work*:

> "Young carers are children and young persons under 18 who provide, or intend to provide, care, assistance or support to another family member. They carry out, often on a regular basis, significant or substantial caring tasks and assume a level of responsibility which would usually be associated with an adult. The person receiving care is often a parent but can be a sibling, grandparent or other relative who is disabled, has some chronic illness, mental health problem or other condition connected with a need for care, support or supervision.
>
> Factors which influence the extent and nature of young carers' tasks and responsibilities include the illness/disability, family structure, gender, culture, religion, income, and the availability and quality of professional support and services."
>
> Becker, S. (2000) 'Young Carers', in Davies, M. (ed.) *The Blackwell Encyclopaedia of Social Work*. Oxford: Blackwell Publishers Ltd, p. 378.

MAKING IT WORK

There is a need to differentiate between the needs of the child as a carer, and the impact of the family illness/disability on the child.

How many young carers are there?

There are no accurate national figures available, but a survey carried out by the Social Survey Division of the Office for National Statistics on behalf of the Department of Health estimates that there are approximately 32,000 young carers aged 8–17 in the United Kingdom, with a lower estimate range of 19,000 and an upper range of 51,000 (Walker, 1996).

The most recent nationwide study was carried out in 1998 by Young Carers Research Group at the University of Loughborough. They undertook a study of 2,203 young carers and found the following:

- The average age of a young carer was 12.
- 86% were of compulsory school age (i.e. 5–15 years old).
- 57% were girls; 43% were boys.
- 14% were from ethnic minority groups.

- 54% lived in lone parent families.
- 58% cared for their mother.
- Tasks performed ranged from basic domestic duties to very intimate care.
- One in three had missed school or had educational difficulties because of their caring role.
- 29% cared for a relative with mental health problems.
- 63% cared for a relative with physical health problems.
- One in five provided intimate care.
- One in four had no external support (other than local young carers' project).

(Dearden and Becker, 1998).

In April 2001, the London Young Carers Workers Forum mapped the demographics of young carers from 21 London projects. The outcome of this exercise showed that of the 2,180 young carers registered with these projects, on average:

- 41% gave primary care
- 50% lived in a lone parent family
- 64% cared for a parent.

(Baker, PRTC, 2002)

The figures above specify lone parent families but also highlight the fact that a significant number of young carers are assisting with care needs in two-parent families.

Types of caring

The tasks undertaken by children and young people vary, according to the nature of the illness or disability, the level and frequency of need for care, the structure of the family unit, etc. A young carer may undertake some or all of the following:

- practical tasks such as cooking, housework and shopping;
- managing the family budget, collecting benefits and prescriptions;
- physical care such as lifting;
- personal care such as dressing, washing, helping with toileting needs;
- giving medication or physiotherapy;
- ensuring safety;
- looking after or parenting younger siblings;
- giving emotional support or worrying;
- interpreting (either because of a hearing, visual or speech impairment or because English is not the first language of the family).

Why do children take caring roles within the family?

Research and practice has shown that children care for a large number of reasons. When there is a person within the family needing care, the child may take on the role of sole or primary carer or may help other adults or siblings with caring tasks. Some choose to take on the task voluntarily, others are informally nominated as a carer and, in some families, it is demanded. The majority, however, just grow into the role.

> *"Helping her is just part of life. I don't really remember it being any different."*
>
> (Young carer)

> *"It's just something I do. It has to be done and there is no one else to do it."*
>
> (Young carer)

> *"There is also the point that some children take it upon themselves to be the 'carer' by virtue of their nature. Maybe this is true in children who are perhaps quite sensitive to the needs of others and more perceptive of the situation. They take a certain responsibility and worry about the parent who is at home whilst they are at school. They feel they should be there with the parent in case they are needed."*
>
> (Disabled parent)

Some of the issues and factors that can lead to a child undertaking inappropriate levels of care are:

- the structure of the family unit
- the nature of the illness and the perception of need
- service provision.

The structure of the family unit

Children may be caring for a lone parent because there is no other able adult in the home who can help with caring needs. In two-parent families children may be caring because the other parent is working in order to support the family financially. They may leave the home early in the morning and not return until evening. These times of day are often when care needs are high (for example, getting dressed, preparing meals), so any caring tasks, including the care of younger siblings, may fall to the young carer.

In some families there may be more than one person who is ill: for example, a child with a disability and a parent with mental ill health, or both parents suffering from different illnesses or conditions.

Adults giving primary care may seek support from children in the family to help manage care needs because of the nature and volume of caring tasks. Some tasks may, for example, require or involve more than one person (lifting, physiotherapy, supervision, ensuring safety). Often caring involves multiple tasks, such as personal care, housework and care of younger children.

Another factor that influences whether a child undertakes inappropriate care tasks or emotional support is whether or not there is a consistent and effective support network from extended family members.

Some parents find it difficult to come to terms with their illness or disability and its consequent impact on children. This is particularly so in the early stages of onset and is frequent among people suffering from mental ill health.

MAKING IT WORK

Recognise that the reasons that children undertake inappropriate levels of care may be complex and that to resolve them may require a multi-faceted approach.

Nature of illness and perception of need

Caring needs vary according to the nature of an illness: whether it is a stable, managed condition, degenerative, or periodic. Periodic episodes and relapses can occur with both physical conditions (e.g. MS, arthritis) and also with mental ill health or substance misuse. Other factors include:

- the speed of onset of the illness;
- the time lags between the onset of the illness, its diagnosis, acceptance of it and seeking help;
- whether or not the person who is unwell or disabled chooses to seek help;
- whether or not the person who is unwell or disabled recognises the level of care their child is giving.

Many families simply do not ask for outside help and as the illness or disability progresses, the caring role gradually increases.

Service provision

Children and young people are known to undertake inappropriate care in families where there is no formal service provision, but also in families where services are being provided but perhaps not in an effectively targeted way or where there is lack of flexibility and frequency.

Families often lack information about services or knowledge about their rights to request assessment. Other factors that affect good provision of services include:

- whether or not an assessment of care needs is effectively and comprehensively carried out (it can often take some time and many visits to assess fully a situation and the family's complete needs);
- whether or not the person who is unwell meets eligibility criteria for services;

- the efficacy, flexibility and speed that statutory services can be delivered to meet all the person's needs;
- whether or not the services can be afforded by the family (if charged).

Families may themselves not wish statutory services to be provided:

- The person who is ill may or may not want a 'stranger' to care for them.
- The family may or may not wish to have external careworkers in the family home.
- Cultural perceptions of illness and disability may mean that help from 'outside' is not expected or wished for, or may not be culturally sensitive.
- Some parents fear that to seek help may result in their children being taken into care.

Emotional impact

Even when all the practical and physical care needs of the person who is unwell or disabled are being met, children still say that they care emotionally and worry about the person. Issues of loss, anger and panic are common feelings experienced by children who live with or help care for a close family member who is ill.

> *"Even if 24-hour care is provided, we are still young people who care. Feelings, emotions and insecurities about parents, brother and sisters do not disappear."*
> (The Children's Society, 2000)

MAKING IT WORK

Recognise that young carers can experience a conflict of emotions which they may not be able to understand or articulate.

There can be a conflict of emotion experienced by many young carers, between feelings of love for the person who is ill, anger at the illness that is affecting them, and resentment about some of the caring responsibilities and lack of adequate external support for the family. All of these, plus a lack of understanding shown by others, can contribute to a roller-coaster of feelings for many children.

> *"It's not just the caring that affects you... What really gets you is the worry of it all. Having a parent who is ill and seeing them in such a state. Of course it's upsetting, you think about it a lot. Someone who is so close to you and so desperately ill is pretty hard to deal with."*
> (Former young carer)

The person who is ill may also develop an emotional dependency on their carer – whether an adult or a child – which cannot be replaced by statutory provision. This has an impact on a child, which they often do not know how to start dealing with on their own.

> *"Mum might be upset after I get home from school and I have to calm her down. But I really don't feel like counselling her."*
> (Young carer)

Long-term effects

Both research and practice has shown that these children and young people may not be experiencing the same life chances as their peers. Their own personal and physical development may be affected, as well as their educational and social opportunities. The impact on their childhood may also impact on adult life, as shown in two recent pieces of research: Frank, Tatum and Tucker, 1999 and Dearden and Becker, 2000.

Both documents state that career opportunities and life chances may be restricted by inappropriate caring responsibilities during childhood. While many young carers have also gained life-skills from their experiences of caring and have developed qualities such as compassion, consideration, determination, empathy and an understanding and tolerance of disability and illness, both pieces of research found that the negative aspects of caring outweighed any positives.

> *"I want to join the army but I'm not leaving her [mum] until my brother is old enough to take care of her."*
> (Young carer)

Frequent effects for children and young people of providing care

- **Problems at school, with completing homework and getting qualifications.**
- **Isolation from other children of the same age and from other family members.**
- **Lack of time for play, leisure, or sport.**
- **Conflict between the needs of the person that they are helping and their own needs, leading to feelings of guilt and resentment.**
- **Lack of recognition, praise or respect.**
- **Feeling that there is nobody there for them, that professionals do not listen to them.**
- **Feelings that they are different from other children.**
- **Feeling that no one else understands their experiences.**
- **Problems moving into adulthood, especially with finding work, their own home, and establishing relationships.**

Children in families where a parent suffers from mental illness can be at risk of developing mental health problems. Around 10,000 children across the country are in this position.

In families where alcohol or drug abuse is a problem, children can be faced with a caring role which can create great anxiety.

(Extract from Department of Health (1999) *Caring about Carers: A National Strategy for Carers.*)

"In some ways it has made it harder for me to get on with friends... When I was 11 they would play with dollies and I'd be cooking and cleaning the house. It makes you feel different and you think they are so childish. Now, at 15, 16, whenever you hear them talk about [their parents] – it's just to complain, 'I want to wear this and she's not washed it!' and you just think they should be grateful... they don't understand."
(Young carer quoted in Surrey Young Carers' Project, 1998)

"When you're younger you don't really understand what's happening. You know this person as your mum and you think, oh yeah I really love my mum. Then suddenly they turn into a totally different person and you can't understand. You're trying to relate what they're doing to the person that you've known all your life and you can't do it, and you get really confused."
(Young carer quoted in Surrey Young Carers' Project, 1998)

"I used to run away from school because I always wanted to be with my mum. I used to think that my mum was going to die. I was about eight... I kept getting told that she was not going to die, but she was not getting any better, which means she is worse – which means she will die. They treated me as if I was playing truant, but I wasn't. ...I just said that I had a feeling inside me they did not understand."
(Young carer quoted in Clark, 1996)

Should we accept the notion of 'young carers'?

It is argued by some (e.g. Wates, M. and Olsen, R.) that the provision of adequate services to the person in need of care will prevent children having to take on inappropriate caring roles for their disabled relative. It is also argued that funds and efforts should be directed towards direct services for disabled adults rather than support targeted at young carers. This perspective has generated a debate about the legitimacy of work to support young carers.

It is important that support and improved practice for young people caring for a disabled parent should not in any way undermine the importance of recognising the rights and needs of disabled parents themselves. Indeed, the debate also needs to recognise the diversity of situations in which parents have rights to support, including:

- parents who have mental ill health, long-term illness, periodic or degenerative conditions and need care in the family home;
- parents who have children with disabilities or who are ill and need care in the family home;
- parents who need support because of misuse of substances.

Young carers exist in a social, economic and political context in which there are a number of tensions and contradictions. For example, is the primary focus the child's or the parent's needs? The voice of the child is important and must be heard, but there should be a balance – the needs of **all** family members should be taken into account.

It would, of course, be ideal not to have children who are caring for family members to such a level that their emotional and physical responsibilities impact on their own development. However, the reality is that it is going to take considerable time and resources to meet effectively and consistently the care needs of all parents who are ill or disabled.

In the meantime, children **do** find themselves in inappropriate caring roles. Many find their own development affected and will benefit from various degrees of support. Through published research and practice, these young people have quite clearly stated their needs, emotions and wishes and what they want to support themselves and their family. It is clear that for as long as children have such needs, best practice should support them.

> *"We wouldn't want to give up caring because we love them too much. If we gave up caring we'd have to change our whole way of life, but we would like help and people to take notice of us."*
>
> (Wiltshire Young Carers' Strategy)

> *"Resources are important and necessary to provide support to our families and us. However, even with 24-hour care, young carers would still exist – we are part of a family and have feelings that need to be recognised – we have all sorts of feelings."*
>
> (The Children's Society, 2000)

Listening to children within a 'whole-family' context

There is a need to move both debate and practice forwards and address how a major shift in attitudes and increased effective service provision for families can be developed. Legislation, guidance and good practice all direct practitioners to consider the needs of the child within the context of the family. A holistic approach is always advocated, meeting the needs of the person who is ill or disabled, recognising family strengths as well as any difficulties or problems and being careful not to undermine parenting skills. Work with young carers and their families should follow such guidelines.

It is also equally important to ensure that, within such a holistic approach, children's voices and feelings are heard and taken into account. Society has a duty to consult, inform, support and protect children who find themselves in a caring role, which impacts upon their own development and aspirations. Children need to also be informed that they have a choice in whether or not to take on a caring role.

MAKING IT WORK

- **Improve practice and increase effective service provision for families.**
- **Continue raising awareness of needs.**
- **Improve consultation with the whole family.**
- **Acknowledge and assess young carers' needs, and offer appropriate support.**
- **Young carers should be informed, consulted and given choices about whether or not they wish to care and, if so, how they wish to be identified and supported.**

The impact of caring on a child

The following four case studies illustrate some of the situations in which young carers may find themselves, the roles they have to play within their families and the effects this may have on them.

Case study 1

Danielle (aged eight) and Petra (aged ten) are sisters. Their mother, Ella, has a history of anxiety which has recently become more severe and she no longer feels able to leave the house. Their father has a full-time job which involves long hours and he is now the only breadwinner. He has found it difficult to understand Ella's illness. Danielle and Petra often miss days of school, as they do not want to leave their mother alone in the house. On one occasion Danielle and Petra came home and found Ella unconscious, having taken an overdose. Petra rang for an ambulance and looked after Danielle until it came. Ella now attends a day centre. She is very open with her daughters about her feelings and they are often her shoulders to cry on.

The school is aware that Ella is ill, but the family have not wanted to share any details. Some of the teachers are more understanding than others about late or unfinished homework. The daughters do not want their friends to find out about their mum and are quite withdrawn at school, occasionally experiencing bullying as a result. They now attend a young carers' club once a fortnight. Club workers describe them as quiet, but both enjoy the break. The carers' organisation providing support to the family are also attempting to support the father with his issues and concerns.

Mental illness is one of the more difficult illnesses to understand. It is not something that manifests in a visible disability, but it is nevertheless very disabling for the sufferer. There are also people who suffer mental health problems but who have not been assessed by health or social services, either because they refuse this facility, or because their illness has not actually been identified. In situations such as this, there is a grave possibility that the young carers will go unrecognised.

Case study 2

Robin is 15 and his sister, Vicky, is 11. Their mother, Pauline, is in her 30s and suffered a stroke 18 months ago. This severely affected her mobility and speech. Her relationship with her partner broke down shortly afterwards and the family moved into council accommodation. Pauline was unable to get out of bed to use the toilet unassisted, so Robin had to get up during the night to help her. This led to academic and behavioural problems at school, where Robin was increasingly socially isolated. There were concerns about the physical well-being of both Robin and Vicky, as they were both engaged in lifting Pauline and her wheelchair, as well as carrying out all household tasks including shopping, cleaning, cooking and gardening.

Both Robin and Vicky felt they had a very close and loving relationship with their mother and the family were reluctant to let strangers into the house to carry out personal care for Pauline, especially as they considered home careworkers provided by Social Services unreliable or insensitive. Pauline was only entitled to night-time care from the Adults and Older People (A&OP) Business Unit of Social Services once a week. She was offered the use of incontinence aids for night-time use but considered this inappropriate. The Children and Families Unit felt that services needed by an adult should be provided by A&OP, even though the intention was to ease the burden on a young person. This disagreement was never settled.

Eventually, Pauline recovered enough to be able to use guide rails and a commode. Robin and Vicky both attend young carers' evening clubs, activities and adventure weekends. Pauline feels they have developed more confidence and was particularly pleased that Robin brought a friend from the young carers' club home for a sleepover. This was the first time he had let a friend meet his mother. Robin also received mentoring from a young carer worker during school time and his behaviour showed a marked improvement.

MAKING IT WORK

All children and young people have a right to be supported and to have choices in determining what constitutes appropriate support.

Strokes can cause very obvious physical disabilities which, for a young carer, can be an embarrassment in front of their friends. Consequently, this feeling of embarrassment can stir up emotions of guilt, anger and frustration. Equally they love their parent and worry about their illness and so have a turmoil of emotions with which to contend.

Case study 3

Jake, 16, comes from a large family who have moved around the country frequently. He is the youngest of four brothers. Both his parents have become increasingly reliant on heroin. All his brothers left home at early ages, having had contact themselves with police, Youth Offending Teams (YOT) and substance misuse organisations. Jake's parents have periods where they are in work and take responsibility for Jake and household duties, but also periods of heavy drug use. They have intermittent contact with support agencies. Social services are aware of the family and are "monitoring the situation" but Jake and his parents do not welcome their support and they feel they do not have enough evidence of need to intervene more assertively.

Jake does not like the unpredictability of his parents' binges, when he has to take charge of cooking, shopping, budgeting, household tasks and taking care of his parents when they are under the influence of heroin. He resents these responsibilities but expresses his anger outside the home. He has an Educational Social Worker whom he does not like and is known to the local YOT. He is not keen on group activities but he does accept one-to-one listening/mentoring sessions from a young carer worker, who is able to take a less formal and authoritarian role than other professionals he has contact with. The young carer worker has liaised with school on Jake's behalf to gain more flexibility in his choice of GCSEs and to enable him to access work experience, as he was finding it difficult to plan his own future. His motivation to achieve his chosen goals has increased.

MAKING IT WORK

Recognise that in families where there is misuse of drugs or alcohol, needs may be different and may change with time. Services therefore need to be flexible and reviewed regularly.

Not only is Jake a young carer when his parents are under the influence of drugs, but he may also be considered a child 'at risk'. As Jake is an older child, about to choose his GCSE subjects, it takes considerable sensitivity on the part of the caring professional to provide the right kind of support without appearing to 'take charge'.

Case study 4

Tim is 16 and has Asperger's Syndrome. His behaviour is often aggressive, unpredictable and destructive. Tim's sister Gemma plays an important part in helping her mother manage his behaviour. She helps to "keep an eye on" Tim and occupies him when he comes home from the day centre. She also helps when Tim has a dentist's or doctor's appointment by going with him and their mother and "doing it first", which makes it easier for Tim to carry out tasks or activities that he is unaccustomed to. Gemma gives up a lot of her free time to help with tasks such as cooking, shopping and cleaning, as her mother is often occupied with supporting Tim.

Their mother is very protective of Tim, has exacting standards for his care and is often in conflict with statutory service providers. Gemma attends a young carers' club and a worker has helped her to take part in a carers' assessment, which was specially designed by young carer workers and young carers themselves. The assessment was carried out by the family's social worker from the Children with Disabilities Unit of Social Services. Gemma is also bullied at school. Through the assessment, Gemma identified that she needed a listener from outside the family as well as more time with her mother without Tim present. There is a conflict between this need and Tim's reluctance to take part in new activities.

MAKING IT WORK

Recognise that some children give significant levels of care to a disabled sibling.

Young carers of siblings can often feel resentment that they do not get the same kind of attention from their parents, even though they understand why more attention must be paid to the disabled child. Experiencing bullying at school adds to the negative feelings of rejection. Again, the child may experience a conflict of emotions: love for their sibling versus resentment or anger at the condition or disabilty. Having a chance to talk through these emotions can be a great help.

Caring for a brother or sister

Some children and young people give significant practical and physical help to siblings who are disabled or chronically ill. Many find themselves with the responsibility of ensuring safety and supporting other needs, for example, where a brother or sister has a learning disability. Others give significant emotional support to parent carers.

Emotional support to a sibling is also a feature of caring for many. Just as in any family, sources of emotional understanding and support are often provided by a sibling, particularly during adolescence.

> *"At times being a carer is soul destroying. I battle against an invisible disease in my brother that means his health deteriorates...I am the only one who can give him emotional support when he is feeling down. It's me who's left to make him smile. However much hard work it is to achieve this, it's always worthwhile for the smiles and looks he gives me."*
> (Source: Bibby and Becker. 2000)

There are also siblings who are not involved in giving significant care but may find their own lives impacted upon by the care needs of the disabled or sick child in a range of ways, such as:

- lack of parental attention due to the care needs and demands of the disabled sibling;
- feelings of embarrassment, resentment, anger and fear towards the sibling with a disability which cannot be easily expressed within the family;
- over-protectiveness towards the sibling with a disability, resulting in them taking on more responsibility than their peer group;
- protecting their parents from some of the care by taking it on themselves;
- an inability to take part in normal family activities due to the disability of their sibling.

> *"We are like two families...someone has to be with [disabled child] all the time while the other [parent] is with the other two children."*
> (Parent carer)

Source: *Information about Siblings* (Southampton Voluntary Services Young Carers' Project)

> *"I don't know what's going to happen when my parents die. I've discussed it with my brother and we may get a house together when we're older and look after her."*
> (Wiltshire Young Carers' Strategy)

The experiences of the children quoted above echo the work undertaken by Atkinson and Crawforth (1995), which records the findings of a study of 29 siblings who were interviewed aged between eight and 16 years. All of them said they helped in some way to care for their brother and sister and they all spoke about their sibling with love and affection. 60% reported that they did not mind helping, the remainder made no comment. Disruption to family life, bullying, public attitudes to disability and difficulties at school were recorded alongside the need for their help in providing care for a brother or sister.

Young carers from Black communities and other cultures

In addition to sharing the specific experiences of all young carers, those from Black communities and other cultures face particular issues:

- The families may be less likely to contact social services departments for fear that their children will be taken away.
- Children from these groups are more likely to be excluded from school.
- Children from these groups are often expected to take responsibility for interpreting for the person they are caring for, regardless of whether or not they understand the issue or it is appropriate to their age.

(Source: Department of Health, 1999c)

Additionally, children from these groups may:

- be less able to access information about services;
- be less able to articulate needs;
- experience racial discrimination as well as discrimination due to disability or illness;
- face cultural interpretations of illness and disability, which may manifest as discrimination or an unwillingness to understand or accept disability.

Families in these communities may feel uncertain about support from formal sources because of cultural expectations of their role and a perception of their duty to look after their elders.

> *"They don't understand it. I've tried to explain it. There's a chemical unbalance in her brain, sort of made it technical so they would accept it more, but they don't. I don't know, I think it's in the Asian Community it's sort of laughed upon, something to hide, I don't think they can admit it."*
> (Young carer aged 17 quoted in Shah and Hatton, 1999)

- None of the families received regular, adequate or appropriate support services.
- Experiences of social services, health services and schools showed a lack of understanding of the problems families faced.
- There were examples of discrimination by race and /or disability.

Source: Jones, Jeyasingham and Rajasooriya, 2002

MAKING IT WORK

Recognise that families from Black communities and other cultures may face 'double discrimination' because of their race and disability.

Poverty and social exclusion

Illness or disability can affect anyone, regardless of their social background or where they live. As discussed below (p. 24) service provision for the person in need of care and for young carers themselves varies from one Local Authority and Health Trust to another. Having someone who is ill or disabled can put constraints on family life, and caring responsibilities place further constraints on the carer, whether they are an adult or a child. Families who are on low incomes or who rely on benefits face further constraints. Other factors, which can further lead to social exclusion and impact on both the family and carers, are:

- poverty of environment (e.g. locality of housing, provision and access to resources);
- lack of regular, accessible and affordable transport (a particular issue for families living in rural communities);
- inadequate and inappropriate housing;
- extra costs incurred (e.g. heating, laundry, taxi fares to appointments);
- cost of services, if charged, to the person in need of care;
- stigma associated with illness or disability (e.g. mental ill health, alcohol dependency, learning disability);
- carers from Black communities and other cultures may face even more limited access to financial resources (Howard, 2001) and may face racism and culturally insensitive services;
- socially, many young carers say that they find it difficult to go out, make friends or invite friends to their family home;
- attending school trips or after-school activities can also be difficult, both in financial terms and in feeling able safely to leave the person who needs care;
- some young carers feel compelled to stay at home instead of leaving to go to higher education or employment; others leave earlier than they might have chosen because they find it too emotionally or physically demanding to stay.

> *"Means tested benefits are not good. They look at income, not outgoings."*
>
> (Disabled parent quoted in The Children's Society, 2000)

MAKING IT WORK

Recognise that families where someone is ill or disabled and on a low income face further constraints which may increase social exclusion.

Personal issues/relationships

The following quotes are taken from *Young Carers and Our Families* (The Children's Society, 2000):

> "We are members of a family and have emotions and concerns related to caring responsibilities that need to be understood."
>
> "It can be very difficult to invite friends back to our homes. This can lead to us feeling isolated and it can be very depressing and lonely. Having a boyfriend/girlfriend (inviting them home, having time to go out, and spending time together) can be very difficult."
>
> "We would like more opportunities to go out, meet others and make friends who understand. Young carers' projects really help us to do this."
>
> "We would also like the person we are caring for to have more chances to go out and do things and not be stuck indoors all day."
>
> "It would help our families and us if there were a greater awareness of the extent, role and responsibilities of young carers in society generally. There also needs to be a better understanding of the needs of people with disabilities, mental health difficulties and illness. Society needs to be more accepting. It could happen to anyone!"

MAKING IT WORK

Recognise that young carers may not have the same opportunities to socialise as their peers.

Loss and bereavement

Young carers may experience a sense of loss in a number of ways, which may need support and understanding.

> *"Since the accident, she's changed...she's just not my mum anymore."*

This is also true for the person in need of care and other family members.

> *"I used to play football with them on Saturdays. Now I can't even get down the hill to watch."*
> (Father)

Many young carers may experience bereavement, and their needs for information and support may need to be met by an appropriate agency during this time.

Current support and services for young carers and their families

Service provision for the person in need of care and for young carers themselves varies according to the Local Authority or Health Trust, which administers the area. Most Local Authorities highlight the need to identify and support young carers and have policies that are based on the Children Act and Quality Protects Framework. Some Health Authorities have included guidance for provision in their Health Improvement Plans but the majority have not (Brunt, 2000).

Families may often require services or support from a number of agencies, including Health, Social Services and Housing. Young carers may also need support from education services. There is therefore a need for practice to reflect the guidance that recommends inter-agency and inter-departmental working (see Chapters 2 and 5).

The Fair Access to Care Services Guidance (Department of Health, 2002) on eligibility criteria for adult social care provides councils with a framework for determining eligibility for adult social care to be used for all adult service users. By using the framework, implementation should lead to fairer access to care services across the country. The primary purpose of the Guidance is to ensure that adults with social care needs receive appropriate, effective and timely help that promotes their independence. The Guidance also makes clear the need for joint assessment and provision of services when **both** adult and children's services are involved. In addition, it states that, "In the course of assessing an individual's needs, councils should recognise that adults, who have parenting responsibilities for a child under 18 years, may require help with these responsibilities."

MAKING IT WORK

Ensure that all agencies involved with supporting families where there is a member in need of care, are able to identify if a child is undertaking inappropriate levels of care and the procedures that need to be implemented in order to support the child and family.

Young carers and benefit entitlements

Invalid Care Allowance (ICA) and Income Support can be available to young carers aged 16 and over. To receive ICA they need to be providing care for more than 35 hours per week but not studying for more than 21 hours a week. The Carers and Disabled Children Act 2000 has given local councils the power to make direct payments to carers (including 16- and 17-year-old carers receiving support under the Act) to meet their own assessed needs as a carer.

There is no provision for financial assistance to young people aged 16 or over to attend Sixth Form College or further education. Therefore the conflict in financial terms between a child staying at home and receiving benefits and the family struggling to find extra money to enable the child to attend further education is self-evident.

MAKING IT WORK

Ensure that young people over 16 with caring responsibilities are offered real choices in accessing further education.

The needs of disabled parents

A Jigsaw of Services (Department of Health, 2000) recommends a major shift in the approach to working with disabled parents. This includes a recognition of the right of disabled people to be supported in fulfilling their roles and responsibilities as parents, and the development of policies and strategies to improve 'joined-up working' across adults' and children's service divisions and between agencies.

Services to families who have a disabled child or chronically sick child receive services if they meet the eligibility criteria under the 1989 Children Act. However, as previously discussed, many families do not meet eligibility criteria and so do not receive services. Others may be unaware of help available or, if means tested, may not choose to pay for services.

Direct work with young carers

Projects have evolved across the UK to meet local needs and offer a range of direct services to young carers and their families. Information, advocacy and support are also offered to families by most projects. Some projects are managed by national organisations (e.g. The Princess Royal Trust for Carers, Barnardo's, NCH, Crossroads for Carers). Others are independently funded and locally managed, many relying on small voluntary incomes and supported by Children in Need, Community Fund (formerly the National Lottery Charity Board) or Comic Relief. The development of independent projects has in some cases been rather 'ad hoc' according to local awareness, commitment and resources.

Some projects have formal service agreements and core funding from local authorities, but this does not apply to all. Nevertheless, young carers' projects have been greatly valued by both the children and their families and have developed a range of expertise that is reflected in the wide range of needs-led services. Projects have also played a key role in raising awareness and identifying gaps in services. Crucially, this is not only for young carers but also for the people in need of care.

The work of young carers' projects is discussed in detail in Chapter 7.

Education

Schools, the Youth Service and Connexions Services have a key role to play in supporting young carers. This is explored in detail in Chapter 5.

Access to information

As with provision of services, access to information also varies according to where people live, with each Local Authority and Health Trust producing its own material. It is hoped that this guide will highlight the type of information and services that meet the identified needs of young carers and their families. The Young Carers Initiative Website offers information to young carers, their families and those who work with them. A list of other useful websites can be found on pages 54–55 of this guide.

Young Carers Initiative Website
www.childrenssociety.org.uk/youngcarers

Chapter 3 looks in more detail at the assessment process for young carers and their families.

Section 2

Putting it into Practice

CHAPTER 2
The Voice of Young Carers

Young Carers' Festivals

Young Carers' Festivals are jointly organised by The Children's Society and South East Hampshire YMCA (Fairthorne Manor) and enable large numbers of young carers to take part in consultations about their own needs and those of their families. The first Young Carers' Festival was organised in 2000, when 640 young carers from all over the UK came together for the first time. In 2001 and 2002, more than 1,200 young people aged 10–17 attended. From the outset there was a commitment to offer consultation methods that were participatory and fun, in order to fit in with the festival mood. Yet, equally important was the need to ensure children and young people were given the chance to relax, have fun and socialise.

The Festivals provide opportunities for young carers to say how they would like services to meet more effectively their needs and the needs of their families. The young carers have given some clear messages for policy and practice, which are reflected throughout this guide. Many of their requests for ways in which services could be improved are given below. But the young people also expressed a number of clear and basic needs – echoing the voices of young carers in many other pieces of research – that are important for all agencies working with young carers to take on board.

At the first Festival, in 2000, the young people told us what they thought schools should do to help them. Comments included:

> *"Better understanding towards disability and carers. It hurts our feelings when someone says something about our families."*
>
> *"Find out more about young carers so that teachers understand and are aware of the situation at home."*
>
> *"We also need attention and caring for."*

They also wanted all agencies and government to recognise them and listen.

> *"We need our voice heard, not next week or tomorrow but now!"*

Young carers at the second Young Carers' Festival, in 2001, told us that:

- more flexible and faster responses are needed from health and social services;
- it takes too long to assess families' needs;

- care packages are not always flexible enough to respond to any changes or to illnesses that are episodic in nature;
- assessments and service care planning also need to include thought about crisis provision, should it be required.

Consultation at the second festival produced a top-ten list of priorities in answer to the question: "What would make life easier for you and your family?":

- Better funding (long-term) for the Young Carers' Projects
- For people to know your situation but not to treat you any differently (no discrimination)
- Access to phones at school in case of an emergency at home
- Better places for disabled people on holiday – like a holiday, not an institution
- Someone to come and help my mum so that I can have a break
- Easy access to open places for disabled people
- More disability awareness
- Information on who to turn to for help with family and individual problems
- Transport help
- More places for young carers to go at any time.

Following the second festival, four young carers went as representatives of the Festival to the House of Lords to give a presentation to the All Party Parliamentary Group for Children. Points made by the young carers in an impressive presentation included the following:

- Agencies need to recognise that it is vital to consult with young carers and their families because they know their situation best.
- Young carers want schools to respect and understand the issues they have to deal with at home and to promote more awareness and tolerance of disability and illness.
- Young carers want health services to communicate to them about the medical care of parents or siblings in a clear and simple way, e.g., what to expect in the way of illness or behaviour, what to do in case of emergency.
- Young carers want social workers to understand that all families are different and that it is important to consider all the family members and their needs, not just one member. They want social workers to provide flexible services because circumstances can change, affecting the level of support young carers need.

The politicians present were clearly impressed by what the young people had to say and agreed to make sure that the government departments concerned also heard these messages. Following the young carers' presentation, a question was asked in the House of Lords on 19th November 2001: "How do government policies in education support the needs of young carers?"

During the debate, it was announced that the Government would set up a group, which has now been convened, within the Department for Education and Skills to see what more can be done to support young carers in schools. It was very rewarding for the young people to know that the hard work they had all put into consultation at the Festival has been acknowledged and is being taken forward so positively by Parliament.

At the third Festival in 2002, the young people's Festival planning group took consultation a step further and invited three MPs, (representing each major political party) to attend a Question Time session organised during the Festival. Again the focus of the young people's concern was around the lack of understanding and coherent provision of support for them and their families.

The Festivals have enabled young carers to have a coherent voice at a national level, but it is equally important to remember to consult with them at all levels of practice (see pages 55–56).

MAKING IT WORK

Young carers say they wish to be listened to, understood and believed. They also wish to be valued, consulted, respected.

CHAPTER 3
Assessments

> *"Assessments are also important in order to meet the needs of us and our families. When doing an assessment it is important to understand how the condition or illness can affect the whole family and how families' needs and individuals' needs may differ but also affect each other."*
>
> (Young carer quoted in The Children's Society, 2000)

This chapter focuses specifically on the assessment of the needs of young carers and the people for whom they are caring. It provides guidance and information to help promote consistent and co-operative practice across a wide variety of agencies. Inter-agency practice and strategies are discussed further in terms of service provision in Chapter 4.

Pro-active intervention

Young carers may often be difficult to identify and many do not seek help until a crisis is reached. It is important that strategies are in place so that families requiring assistance with a person's care needs feel able to seek help before this point. All agencies therefore need to be proactive and consider how best:

a) to identify and reach out to families in order to offer support to prevent inappropriate care being undertaken by children;

b) to intervene if it is evident that this is already happening;

c) to provide direct support to young carers.

MAKING IT WORK

Procedures need to be in place so that the same principles are followed whatever route is taken to gain access to an assessment and to other services. This will require planning and collaboration between agencies and adults' and children's services at both strategic and service provision levels.

The role of the health service

Although social services departments have a major role to play in supporting young carers and their families, they may not be the key agency for initially identifying needs. The National Strategy for Carers (Department of Health, 1999c) states that GPs and other primary care staff, in particular, can provide valuable, sensitive support to young carers and their families. Health is likely to be a key agency that a family turns to for help with an illness or disability. Therefore it is important that questions are asked by health professionals about who is providing support and meeting care needs in the home and, if necessary, that the family is directed to sources of help or referred for an assessment of need. Such timely intervention could help prevent children undertaking inappropriate levels of care.

"I quite often go in with my mother when she goes to the doctor but they still don't recognise the fact that I'm a young carer and still don't pay attention or give time to that matter. So you can't say they don't recognise it because it is obviously there."

(Young Carers' Festival 3)

The National Health Service Priorities Guidance (Department of Health, 1999d) states that GP surgeries must have registers for identifying carers, including young carers. Bibby and Becker (2000) suggest health agencies keep an up-to-date family tree in health records to assist with identification of who provides care in the family. School nurses also have a role to play in early identification and intervention (McLure, 2001) (see Chapter 5 for information on the role of schools).

The following are recommendations to health professionals presented by Baker, PRTC (2002):

MAKING IT WORK

Health agencies need to ensure that training and information are given to all relevant practitioners so that they can identify young carers and offer or signpost the family to appropriate support.

Look beyond the patient and into the home

- If a patient is discharged from hospital and is known to have a long-lasting illness and/or disability for which they require care, do not assume there to be an adult at home to care for them.
- Ask the patient/client if there are children in the family who may be affected by their change in health status, and if they could be referred to the local young carers' project for support.
- If a young person attends a doctor's or hospital appointment with a patient/client, ask what level of support that young person gives to the patient/client. Ask the patient/client if they would consider alternative arrangements so as to avoid the young person accompanying them to such appointments. Also ask what support the patient/client may require to avoid or reduce care given by young people in the family.
- If a family member is diagnosed with a long-lasting illness and/or disability, ask if the patient/client would like other family members to receive age-appropriate information on that illness and/or disability. With approval from the parent(s), provide young carers with age-appropriate information on the condition of the cared-for relative, together with details of any associated voluntary organisations. This may help to alleviate some of the irrational fears young carers can have about a relative's illness and/or disability, through not being given access to, or enough information about the illness and/or disability.

National Service Frameworks and Health Improvement Programmes

National Service Frameworks are being developed in order to improve services and set national standards to improve quality and equality in health and social services care. The Children's National Service Framework will develop new national standards across the National Health Service and social services for children:

- to improve the lives and health of children and young people through the delivery of appropriate, integrated, effective, evidence-based and needs-led services;
- to improve the experiences and satisfaction of children, young people and their carers with the services provided for them.

Health Improvement Programmes (HIMPs) are also part of a strategy to tackle health inequalities. Children's and families' health needs should be considered in these plans in order to lead to statutory service provision. Health providers are key to meeting the needs of young carers and their families. HIMPs should consider how to provide for parenting and family support and how to identify and support young carers.

MAKING IT WORK

Ensure that the needs of young carers and their families are addressed in strategic planning at all levels.

Effective assessments

Delivery of coherent services and support begins with effective assessments. Timely assessments of both the person who needs care and the whole family could prevent a child undertaking inappropriate levels of care in the first place.

Any assessment that is undertaken should focus on:

- **recognising the needs of any young carer;**
- **the whole family;**
- **how the assessment can support the person who needs care, including any parenting support needs.**

The following guidance given in a training guide for working with mentally ill parents and their children is sound practice for all assessors, regardless of the client's specific needs:

- **When gathering information in an assessment, consider the whole professional network and who holds relevant information. Be careful not to subject families to repeated assessments if current information can be gathered, with consent, from another professional.**
- **Make sure that professionals' issues about confidentiality or role boundaries do not prevent an exchange of information which parents and their children want and which would be of benefit to them.**

(Source: Department of Health, 1998)

MAKING IT WORK

Timely assessments of both the person who needs care and the whole family could prevent a child under-taking inappropriate care in the first place.

Statutory services have powers and responsibilities to assess and support young carers under:

- Children Act 1989
- Carers (Recognition and Services) Act 1995
- Carers and Disabled Children Act 2000
- National Service Framework for Mental Health (Standard 6)
- Human Rights Act 1998

...and to recognise young carers and their needs under:

- Quality Protects Initiative (DoH, 1998)
- *Caring About Carers: A National Strategy for Carers* (DoH, 1999c)
- *Young Carers – Making a Start* (DoH, 1996b)
- *National Health Service Priorities Guidance* (DoH, 1999d)
- National Child and Adolescent Mental Health Strategic and Implementation Plan
- *Social Inclusion: Pupil Support (Circular 10/99)* (DfEE, 1999b)
- *National Healthy Schools Standard: Guidance* (DfEE, 1999a)
- *Jigsaw of Services* (DoH, 2000)
- *Fair Access to Care Services* (DoH, 2002)

There is also a need to recognise and, if needed, assess the person who is in need of care under:

- NHS and Community Care Act 1990
- Community Care (Direct Payments) Act 1996
- Sex Discrimination Act 1975
- Disability Discrimination Act 1995
- Chronically Sick and Disabled Persons Act 1970
- National Health Service Act 1977
- Mental Health Act 1983
- Fair Access to Care Eligibility for Services Guidance 2002
- A Jigsaw of Services: Inspection of services to support disabled adults in their parenting role
- Disabled Persons (Services, Consultation and Representation) Act 1986
- Children Act 1989 (for services for disabled children)
- Race Relations (Amendment) Act 2000

Agencies in Scotland, Wales and Northern Ireland will need to refer to legislation and guidance relevant to their country when undertaking assessments.

Assessing the needs of young carers

The key legislation for assessing young carers is the 1995 Carers (Recognition and Services) Act, the 1989 Children Act and the Framework for the Assessment of Children in Need and their Families (Department of Health, Department for Education and Employment, Home Office, 1999), although not all young carers are children in need. Other supporting guidance is outlined later in this chapter.

From: ***Framework for the Assessment of Children in Need and their Families***

3.62
An assessment of family circumstances is essential. Young carers should not be expected to carry inappropriate levels of caring which have an adverse impact on their development and life chances. It should not be assumed that children should take on similar levels of caring responsibilities as adults. Services should be provided to parents to enhance their ability to fulfil their parenting responsibilities. There may be differences of view between children and parents about appropriate levels of care. Such differences may be out in the open or concealed. The resolution of such tensions will require good quality joint work between adult and children's social services as well as co-operation from schools and health care workers. This work should include direct work with the young carer to understand his or her perspective and opinions. The young person who is a primary carer of his or her parent or sibling may have a good understanding of the family's functioning and needs which should be incorporated into the assessment.

3.63
Young carers can receive help from both local and health authorities. Where a child is providing a substantial amount of care on a regular basis for a parent, the child will be entitled to an assessment of their ability to care under section 1(1) of the Carers (Recognition and Services) Act 1995 and the local authority must take that assessment into account in deciding what community care services to provide for the parent.

The National Strategy for Carers (Department of Health, 1999c) states that under the Carers (Recognition and Services) Act 1995:

"Young carers can ask for an assessment of their needs. But many are not aware that this is possible. With the help of the voluntary sector, the statutory services should ensure that young carers are not expected to carry **inappropriate levels of caring responsibility**. To achieve this, disabled or ill parents need support to maintain their independence and to carry out their parenting

MAKING IT WORK

The provision of community care services should ensure that children are not expected to carry out inappropriate caring responsibilities (1995 Carers (Recognition and Services) Act).

MAKING IT WORK

Under the 1995 Carers (Recognition and Services) Act, a young carer's right to an assessment occurs at the time of the user's community care assessment.

responsibilities. Services must consider the needs of all family members including children with caring responsibilities. Sometimes there is a delicate balance to be struck between the rights of a child to have support to reduce the caring burden and the reluctance of some families to accept intervention or support from social services."

The Carers and Disabled Children Act 2000

To implement parts of the National Strategy for Carers, the Carers and Disabled Children Act 2000 gave local councils new powers to support carers flexibly in carrying out their caring responsibilities. It enables councils to make direct payments to carers, including 16- and 17-year-old carers. The guidance does not envisage many situations where such a provision would be the best option for a young carer. In most circumstances it is better to ensure that the person cared for is receiving sufficient services so that the young person is not undertaking a substantial caring role. However, there are a small number of situations where a 16- or 17-year-old is choosing to undertake a substantial caring role for a period – for example, if a parent is terminally ill – where it could be helpful to a young carer to receive a direct payment.

Quality Protects

The Government's Quality Protects Initiative (1998) refers to the need

"to ensure that children whose parents have specific needs arising out of disability or health conditions enjoy the same life chances as all other children in the locality. This requires local authorities to identify children with additional family burdens and to provide services that are geared to ensure these children's education and general development do not suffer."

The UN Convention on the Rights of the Child

It is also important to recognise a child's rights under the United Nations Convention on the Rights of the Child. Both the 1989 Children Act and the United Nations Convention on the Rights of the Child recognise that the views of children should be taken into consideration when decisions are being made about their welfare.

MAKING IT WORK

Where there are children in the family, it is important to establish how the disabled/ill person is assisted with his/her care needs and parenting responsibility and whether or how the children might be helping (1995 Carers (Recognition and Services) Act).

The UN Convention gives guidance on the rights and needs of all children. The sections that are particularly relevant for young carers are:

Articles 9 and 18 The right of a child to live with their parents and that parents have a responsibility for the well-being and upbringing of their child. The state should provide assistance to the parents and help them in any way possible to ensure a healthy upbringing for the child.

Article 12 In all situations, where at all possible, the opinion of the child should be heard and taken into account.

Articles 15 and 31 Children and young people have the right to rest and leisure and to enjoy appropriate play and recreational activities and to participate freely in cultural life and the arts and the right to join groups and clubs.

Article 17 The right to information.

Articles 19 and 28 Children and young people have the right to the best available education and to opportunities to develop their personality, mental and physical ability to their fullest potential.

Meeting the family's needs

"Social workers need to understand that all families are different and that it is important to consider ALL the family members and their needs, not just 'one member'. Please also understand that family and individual circumstances change – the person cared for may not know how they will feel from day to day, or week to week and this affects the level of support we need. Services need to be flexible."

(Quote from parent in The Children's Society, 2000)

The importance of the whole-family approach

Young carers do not care in isolation from the rest of their family. Although they need support for themselves, their needs should also be considered in the context of their whole family.

The practice guidance issued under the 1995 Carers (Recognition and Services) Act for the assessment of young carers states that, "The child should be listened to and his/her views respected." It also advises that, "The needs and strengths of the whole family should be considered when making an assessment and providing services to support the young carer."

Dearden and Becker (2000b) elaborate on the reasoning behind the whole-family approach:

"Young carers' independence cannot be separated from their parents' independence. It is not possible to have true independence for one without independence for the other. Ill and disabled parents need to be supported as parents as well as disabled people, so they can achieve personal independence and control over their own lives and provide the kind of quality of parenting to their children that they wish for. This will enable many families to prevent children from having to take on caring responsibilities in the first place, especially in the absence of any alternatives."
(Dearden and Becker, 2000b)

A whole-family approach to supporting young carers is also echoed in the *Framework for the Assessment of Children in Need and their Families* (Department of Health, Department for Education and Employment and Home Office, 1999).

MAKING IT WORK

- **Think whole family**
- **Think young carer**
- **Think parenting needs**

Financial and environmental issues

Section 2 of the Framework for Assessment Guidance states that assessors should consider environmental factors such as:

- housing (e.g. does it meet needs of disabled family members?)
- income
- accessibility and availability of community resources.

"They should look at outgoings... not just income. Disabled families have a lot of extra expenses!"
(Disabled parent)

"Services should provide sufficient financial support to ensure that young carers and their households do not live in poverty. They should also ensure that young carers do not have to postpone or curtail educational opportunities in order to support their households."
(Shah and Hatton, 1999).

MAKING IT WORK

Assessments of families who live in rural areas will need to include consideration of any extra resources that may be required to enable access to services, and take into account any issues regarding social exclusion.

The Framework for Assessment Guidance also states that staff should:

- take account of experiences of any discrimination in an individual's response to services;
- take account of the barriers that prevent the social integration of families with disabled members;
- avoid using one set of cultural assumptions and stereotypes to understand the child's and their family's circumstances.

When a referral is made for a child who is caring, consider:

- **Is the family member for whom they are caring already receiving services from us?**
- **Is an assessment or review of the person who needs care required?**
- **Is the child's school involved or aware of what is happening (family situation)?**

When a referral is made for an adult or child with a disability or illness, consider:

- **Is there a child in the family who may be helping to provide care?**
- **Have they been offered an assessment?**
- **What can be offered to help the whole family?**
- **Does the parent need support in their parenting role?**

Assessing the needs of the person who needs care, including any parenting support needs

Local health bodies and councils who are operating partnership arrangements under section 31 of the Health Act 1999 should follow the Fair Access to Care Services Guidance (Department of Health, 2002). Its eligibility criteria for adult social care can be used to help determine the starting point for joint packages of continuing health and social care.

In the course of assessing an individual's needs, councils should recognise that adults who have parenting responsibilities for a child under 18 years may require help with these responsibilities.

When drawing up eligibility criteria for adult social care, councils should have regard to the Sex Discrimination Act 1975, the Disability Discrimination Act 1995 (see below), the Human Rights Act 1998, and the Race Relations (Amendment) Act 2000.

MAKING IT WORK

When a referral is received for one family member, it is important to think about the others and their role and needs.

A 'young carer' assessment should trigger an assessment or review of the person who needs care.

MAKING IT WORK

Check that a personal care package not only meets regular individual care needs, but considers the range of tasks that might be needed when professional carers are not present and that may result in the child/ren assuming responsibility.

MAKING IT WORK

Consider how the needs of families who do not meet eligibility criteria for services or who experience episodic illness can be addressed.

Disability Discrimination Act 1995

2.31

Under Part III of the Disability Discrimination Act 1995 (rights of access to goods, facilities and services) service providers, including social services departments and health but not as yet education, must not discriminate against disabled people (including children) by refusing to provide any service which is provided to members of the public, by providing a lower standard of service or offering a service on less favourable terms. These requirements came into force on 2 December 1996.

2.32

Since October 1999, service providers have had to take reasonable steps to:

- change any policy, practice or procedure which makes it impossible or unreasonably difficult for disabled people to make use of services;
- provide an auxiliary aid or service if it would enable (or make easier for) disabled people to make use of services; and
- provide a reasonable alternative method of making services available to disabled people where a physical feature makes it impossible or unreasonably difficult for disabled people to make use of them.

2.33

From 2004 service providers will have to take reasonable steps to remove, alter or provide reasonable means of avoiding physical features that make it impossible or unreasonably difficult for disabled people to use the services.

From: *Framework for the Assessment of Children in Need and their Families* (Department of Health, 2000: p27)

A Jigsaw of Services

Examples of good practice highlighted in *A Jigsaw of Services: Inspection of services to support disabled adults in their parenting role* (Department of Health, 2000) include:

- **direct payment schemes;**
- **multi-purpose centres which provide a range of services;**
- **assessment form with prompts to guide workers to undertake holistic assessments;**
- **disabled parents and their children enabled to engage, contribute, be understood and understand what was happening through the use of specialist help, peer support and advocates.**

MAKING IT WORK

Adults' and children's and families' services need to communicate and work together.

A Jigsaw of Services also identified a number of disabled parents who were frightened to ask for services because they feared that their children would be taken into care. It stated that the Government wants to ensure that the most appropriate and cost-effective support to meet assessed needs is made available to disabled adults in their parenting role. Services provided should assist the parent and enhance, *not undermine*, the parents' authority, and parents need to be reassured of this.

The report sets out areas that need to be considered in order to offer more flexible and responsive services. This includes acknowledging

"... the changing needs of disabled parents brought about:

- simply through the passage of time and the changing developmental needs of children;
- because of the deteriorating nature of the disabled parents' impairment;
- by changes in the family's circumstances;
- by the parents' ability to recognise and accept their strengths and areas of limitations."

Good practice and innovative policy by some local authorities was highlighted in *Supporting disabled adults in their parenting role* (Wates, 2002) including the following:

- **Establishing routine and co-ordinated procedures for the early identification of disabled adults with parenting responsibilities, with a view to addressing support needs at an early stage.**
- **Ring-fenced, pooled budgets agreed by adults' and children's divisions to support disabled parents who would not otherwise meet standard thresholds for services.**
- **Stipulating that a 'young carer' assessment must automatically trigger a community care assessment of the disabled parent's support needs. (NOTE: This should be extended to all parents who need care.)**

MAKING IT WORK

Cohesive effort is needed at all levels to promote more positive images of illness and disability and provide a safe environment for families to feel able to seek help.

The remainder of this chapter discusses the assessment of young carers in many different family situations.

Language and cultural needs

Ensure that any need for professional interpreters is properly addressed (including when working with young carers in refugee families). It is also important to be sensitive to cultural perceptions and needs around disability, illness and caring whilst recognising a child's fundamental rights to a safe and secure childhood.

The Black Carers Network recommends that suitably trained, culturally competent and anti-racist staff undertake assessments and that local and health authorities work towards promoting racial equality and meeting the requirements of the Race Relations (Amendment) Act 2000 (Powell, 2002).

It is not considered good practice to expect children to interpret for family members, particularly where there is an illness involved.

MAKING IT WORK

Agencies and projects need to find opportunities to make links with front-line workers who have specific responsibilities with Black communities and other cultures.

Refugees and asylum-seekers

The specific needs of refugees and asylum-seekers must be considered when undertaking any assessments. Many arrive in trauma or experiencing mental distress, illness or disability.

Dispersal to inappropriate locations, poverty, social exclusion and racism all diminish the quality of life for refugee children in families. It is important to listen and respond to what asylum-seekers have to say about how to make settlement more effective in order for any dispersal system to work. This means providing adequate support systems (including health services). Children should not be expected to act as interpreters for their parents. Neither should children be expected to give inappropriate levels of care to family members who are ill, disabled or experiencing mental distress. (Based on the response (2002) by the Refugee Children's Consortium to the Home Office White Paper *Secure Borders, Safe Haven*)

When assessing the level of support and services needed by refugee families, it should be remembered that they will not have the kind of support from extended family or community that the host population may have. Nor will they be familiar with the range of services that may be available to help. They may also be unaware of their rights to health care.

- All asylum-seekers and refugees are entitled to primary health care services. All are also entitled to secondary care, except unsuccessful applicants for asylum whose entitlement will be decided based on individual complete circumstances.
- Asylum-seekers are not required to show official documentation when they register with a general practice. A Home Office letter, bill or letter addressed to the asylum applicant will suffice.

(Source: *Health services for asylum-seekers and refugees: Refugee Council Briefing*, July 2002)

MAKING IT WORK

All staff at National Asylum Support Service (NASS) should be aware of issues regarding disability and illness and where to refer for relevant assessment procedures.

Assessing the needs of young carers of parents with mental ill health

A focus of the Child and Adolescent Mental Health (CAMHS) Strategic and Implementation Plan is to support children whose parents have mental ill health. The programme provides the opportunity for CAMHS to assess their services against a set of national standards for good practice and management for CAMHS, which are based

Website
www.hqs.org.uk/NHS/CAMHS.htm

on, and driven by, the needs of children and their families. A key component of the programme is external peer review by teams of experienced professionals who themselves work in CAMHS.

The National Service Framework for Mental Health (Standard 6) states that carers of service users who provide regular and substantial care for a person on Care Programme Approach (CPA) should:

- **have an assessment of their caring, physical and mental health needs, repeated on at least an annual basis;**
- **have their own written care plan which is given to them and implemented in discussion with them;**
- **be involved in their own assessment and care planning process which takes into account the state of their own mental and physical health needs and ability to continue to care.**

Assessing the needs of children of alcohol- and drug-dependent parents

When assessing this group of children, it is important to listen to the perspective of the child and how the impact of their parents' dependency is affecting their well-being and development. Their caring responsibilities may be difficult to identify and quantify but, in addition to practical tasks such as preparing food, household duties and personal care, they may include: ensuring the safety of their parents; looking after younger siblings; giving emotional support; feelings of anxiety.

From: *Drug-Using Parents: Policy guidelines for inter-agency working* (Local Government Association, 1997)

In households where there is drug use, drug agencies should ask questions about children and child care arrangements in each assessment and regularly review these.

Where there is concern, social services need to consider:

- **the child's physical safety, while drug (and alcohol) use is taking place;**
- **possible trauma to the child resulting from changes in parents' moods or behaviour;**
- **the impact of parents' drug use on the child's development, including their emotional and psychological well-being, education and friendships;**
- **the extent to which parental drug use disrupts normal daily routines and prejudices the child's healthy physical and emotional development;**

- any relevant information health care professionals (health visitors, school nurses, community psychiatric nurses) may have;
- the impact on the child of being in a household where illegal activity is taking place, particularly if the home is used for drug dealing;
- how safely the parents' drugs are stored.

On the basis of this, professionals can identify the needs of the child and find ways to meet these and provide support to the family.

If, in spite of support provided to the family, it is felt that the child may be at risk, child protection procedures should be followed. Ideally, each social services workplace should have a named specialist on drugs available for advice and to attend child protection conferences where the use of drugs is an issue.

Children at risk

As with all good childcare practice, it is important for family structures to be maintained and supported as far as possible. However, childcare professionals will be aware that there are inevitably cases where young carers may be in situations where their caring role is exploitative and parents are resistant to intervention. There may also be instances where neglect may give cause for concern. Assessment, monitoring and support at an early stage should be seen as good practice in order to prevent such situations arising. Wates (2002) recommends that support for disabled parents in their parenting role should remain on the agenda even when child protection procedures are underway.

The whole-family approach: good practice guidance

Action checklist for achieving a whole-family approach to assessment

- Listen to the child or young person and respect their views.
- Give time and privacy to children who may need this in order to talk about their situation.
- Acknowledge that this is the way the family copes with disability or illness.
- Acknowledge parents' strengths.

- Beware of undermining parenting capacity.
- Consider what is needed to assist the parent in her/his parenting role.
- Consider the needs of the child(ren) arising from caring responsibilities.
- Consider whether the caring responsibilities are restricting the child's ability to benefit from their education.
- Consider whether the child's emotional and social development is being impaired.
- Remember children must be allowed to be children.
- Provide information on the full range of relevant support services, young carers' groups and contact points for further advice or information on specific issues.

Source: *Carers (Recognition and Services) Act 1995 Practice and Guidance*

Further guidance is also given in *Young Carers – Making a Start* (Department of Health, 1996b). It offers the following checklist to help determine the service needs of a young carer and the family, suggesting that assessors may want to ask:

- Is the illness/disability stable or changing: deteriorating or improving?
- Are the helping tasks of the child acceptable within the family/cultural context, and how do other family members help?
- Are the helping tasks required of a personal or practical nature?
- Is the health or welfare of the child impaired because of the tasks undertaken?
- Do financial problems affect the family's ability to deal with the situation (is advice on welfare benefits needed)?
- What is the level of wider family support?
- Does poor housing affect the family's ability to deal with the situation?
- Is the parent/child relationship [parenting] good enough?
- Is the young person making a positive decision to be or not to be a carer?
- Does the family have time, individually and collectively, away from the demands of the illness/disability?
- Is the child able to participate in school/social activities?
- Is the child's social, emotional or behavioural development affected?
- Which parenting tasks is the adult restricted in undertaking and which does s/he want to carry out her/himself?

Ongoing assessment and monitoring

Becker, Aldridge and Dearden (1998) argue that "professional intervention should not end at the point of service delivery to families". They continue by suggesting that, "Some form of beneficent observation or ongoing assessment should be carried out by those professionals who are involved with vulnerable families whose circumstances may be uncertain, in transition or even in crisis (when children have been called upon to care because support services have failed or new and different needs have arisen)."

Providing an assessment at the right time – in the right place

> *"I wish they [agencies] would stop and think and not give us endless paper to fill in – see this department, see that department, go to this panel, visit and revisit..."*
> (Parent and care receiver)

MAKING IT WORK

Involve young carers and their families in the design of assessment processes and materials.

Practice considerations

When carrying out an assessment the following guidelines may be helpful (adapted and condensed from: Becker, S. (2000) 'Carers' in *Research Matters*, October 2000–April 2001 issue, pp. 47–50; and Dearden and Becker, 2000b):

Arrangements before the assessment takes place

- Families should be told formally that an assessment is taking place and should decide with the assessor who will be present.
- Choose a time and venue appropriate to the whole family.
- Consider if an advocate or interpreter is needed so that children and other family members can participate fully.
- Remember to provide any support needed for family members with sensory or speech impairment.
- Offer the children the opportunity to be assessed separately if they wish.

Talking to families

- Recognise that families may be fearful of acknowledging children's caring roles.
- Be cautious about making assumptions.
- Equally, ensure parents do not feel judged when disclosing their child's caring responsibilities.

MAKING IT WORK

Recognise that families where a member has an illness or a disability may be feeling vulnerable. Offer assessments in a supportive manner which enables families to understand the processes, options and potential benefits.

- Acknowledge that families need to cope in different ways and it is often lack of resources, services and sufficient income that result in children needing to provide inappropriate levels of care.

Carrying out the assessment

- Families should be given information about their entitlements, as well as on the full range of services available.
- Local authorities should emphasise an inclusive rather than exclusive approach to eligibility criteria.
- Practitioners should respond to young carers' needs for emotional support and counselling.
- Families may need specialist help to discuss the financial implications and/or assistance towards receiving services.
- Families should be given written confirmation of the results of their assessment and other relevant information, such as named practitioners for future contact and details of review arrangements.
- Families and young carers should be regularly consulted about the quality and appropriateness of services.
- Remember, early interventions can prevent young caring becoming established. Emphasis should be on preventing children from taking on inappropriate caring responsibilities, and stopping them becoming institutionalised once started.

MAKING IT WORK

Offer timely, comprehensive and holistic assessments to help prevent children undertaking inappropriate levels of care and to meet any identified needs that they and their families may have.

CHAPTER 4
Providing Effective Services

The words of the young carers quoted in Chapter 2 make it clear that there are a number of key elements that are important for the provision of effective services:

1. Communication
   – including information and consultation
2. Coherent inter-agency policy, practice, responsibility and provision
3. Emotional support and understanding
4. Effective, sensitive, timely and flexible support and services that address the needs of the whole family

Drawing on the many projects, organisations and schemes that have built up a wealth of expertise in the support of young carers and their families, this chapter addresses each of the above points in turn. It provides information and examples of good practice that will be helpful to practitioners developing or increasing services to meet the specific needs of young carers and their families. Chapter 5 considers support for young carers within schools. Chapter 6 looks at issues facing young carers in particular circumstances and how agencies can meet their needs. Chapter 7 goes on to discuss some of the specialist services provided by young carers' projects to young carers and their families. Guidance on setting up a new service or developing new resources is also included in this chapter.

1. The need for communication

Open communication is crucial to providing appropriate support to young carers and their families. Methods of communication include:

- providing information
- consultation
- involvement in decision-making
- giving choices.

Providing information

"Young people have a right to know what is happening in their family – we should not have to sit outside doors and listen to find out."

(Young carer quoted in The Children's Society, 2000)

Young carers say they value information about the following:

- services for young carers and for the person who is in need of care;
- the illness of the person who is need of care;
- who the various professionals are who may come into the family home and why;
- benefits, money;
- support with education and career choices;
- specific support needs (e.g. counselling);
- health and safety risk assessments (re: lifting, etc in the home);
- coping in a crisis;
- links to other support groups.

"No-one ever sat down and explained to me and my brother what manic depression was. Mum might have done, but no professional person ... if someone had explained what it was, it would have helped."

(Surrey Young Carers, 1998)

"Whenever possible we would like health services to communicate to us about medical care of parents/siblings. Information we are given needs to be easy to understand and only what we need for our family. For example: what to expect in the way of illness or behaviour; what to do in an emergency, who to ring.

GPs need to be honest about medical care. It isn't always easy for parents to explain to children/young people about their conditions/illness. Therefore, GPs need to find a way to do it in accessible and appropriate ways."

(The Children's Society, 2000)

Accessing information

Information for users

Consider where to disseminate information about services for young carers and their families. It is also important that information about family and young carer support is accessible to the person who is ill or disabled. This should be available in a range of appropriate formats, written, visual, braille/audio tapes and in a range of languages. Locations for written information could include:

- GP surgeries
- the point of hospital discharge
- schools – including community information boards
- community centres
- libraries
- churches, temples, mosques and synagogues
- leisure centres
- day centres
- youth clubs

Local media could also be used, if this is done sensitively (include ethnic media, magazines and programmes).

Good practice examples

All projects usually have a good database of information material.

1. **Sutton Young Carers' Project (PRTC) has a library of leaflets, books and videos that are available to the young people.**
2. **Devon Young Carers has produced an information wallet containing information relevant for young carers plus sign-posting to other youth information agencies and resources.**
3. **Skye and Lochalsh Young Carers has produced an information pack, which includes information on signing, basic first aid, effects of alcohol, drugs and descriptions of mental illness.**

MAKING IT WORK

- Children and young people should be offered information about the disability or health problem that is affecting their family member. It needs to be:
  - timely;
  - age-appropriate;
  - jargon-free;
  - accessible in a range of formats and languages.
- Provision of such information should also respect the rights, wishes and dignity of the person who needs care.

Using the Internet

There are a number of websites that have been developed for young carers by local projects (see Bubblycrew website on page 55). National resources include:

The Children's Society website

provides a national focus for young carers and has the following information pages:

- A regularly updated news section on events and developments.
- Information on the Young Carers Initiative, staff and successes so far.
- A general information page, including links to other useful sites with details such as homework help, health advice and local carers' projects.
- A page dedicated to information and links for families.
- A page for professionals, including messages from young carers and their families for social services, health and education.
- A page listing young carers' projects in the UK.

It also invites young carers and their families to send in their views and comments.

The Children's Society website
www.childrenssociety.org.uk/youngcarers

MAKING IT WORK

Ensure that staff and young people are given information about safe surfing and are supervised appropriately when using the Internet.

The Princess Royal Trust website

The website of The Princess Royal Trust for Carers is intended to be a resource for any carer, as well as providing specific advice to particular groups of carers such as young carers. The site's lively discussion boards and chat rooms are a valuable resource to carers, giving them an opportunity to reflect on what it is like to be a carer, and to share their experiences with others. The search facility allows carers to find their nearest Princess Royal Trust Carers' Centre, or to look for recent news stories, and the site provides links to hundreds of other relevant websites and organisations.

The young carers' section of the site deals with issues such as stress, schoolwork, bullying, and isolation. There are links through to those young carers' projects in the Trust that have created their own websites specifically for young carers. Other areas of the site include information on caring for someone with a specific condition, as well as tips on how to look after yourself.

The Princess Royal Trust website
www.carers.org

Carers UK

The Carers UK website provides a gateway for young carers seeking access to information about their rights and the support that is available to them.

The Carers UK website
www.carersonline.org.uk

Young Carers Research Group, Loughborough University

This site has details of all YCRG publications (including an order form), an annotated bibliography of other publications and articles on young carers, contact details for members of the YCRG, details of young carers' projects in the UK, and much more.

The YCRG website
www.ycrg.org.uk

Good practice example: Bubblycrew website

A website has been created by the Bubblycrew (Hammersmith and Fulham Young Carers) based on their experiences and to highlight their issues and concerns, as well as giving a voice and support to other young carers. Young people were involved throughout in both design and content, learning new skills as well as finding a new medium for getting their voices heard. The Bubblycrew won first prize in the Cable and Wireless Childnet International Awards 'Not for Profit Category'. The judges said, "This a very moving website, which tackles a sensitive issue in a positive way".

Bubblycrew have also made a video to be used in schools (see page 88).

The Bubblycrew website
www.bubblycrew.org.uk

MAKING IT WORK

Add relevant websites to your organisation's websites (including schools). Encourage staff to use the site to update policy and practice and to make sites accessible to young people.

The need for consultation

One child's quote made at a presentation to the All Party Parliamentary Group for Children at the House of Lords 2001 encapsulates the importance of remembering to consult:

"When people do something without asking, it won't be right."

The rights of children and young people to be consulted routinely about how services which affect them are developed and delivered is enshrined in the UN Convention on the Rights of the Child, Article 12 (see page 39).

There is a need to ensure that children's voices and feelings are heard and taken into account. All agencies have a duty to consult, inform, support and – if necessary – protect children who find themselves in a caring role, which might have an impact on their development and aspirations (The Children's Society, 2002). Consultation needs to avoid tokenism and have meaning and authenticity for young people. Feedback is an important part of consultation.

Consultation with young carers and their families has a vital role to play in developing coherent, effective services to meet needs. Good consultation should empower children and their families to make decisions and choices and also enable them to feel more able and confident to approach agencies for help when it is needed.

Consultation needs to be taken at all levels:

- to meet the needs of individual families;
- to influence local policy, practice and service delivery;
- to influence national policy and guidance.

Young carers who have accessed projects say they have appreciated being consulted about policy and services for themselves and their families. This has happened at a local level and at a national level, such as the Young Carers' Festivals jointly organised by YMCA and The Children's Society (see Chapter 2).

MAKING IT WORK

Key principles of consultation

- **Consult with an open mind.**
- **Involve children in planning the consultation.**
- **Give feedback.**
- **Show respect for child or young person.**
- **Make consultation flexible, enjoyable and meaningful.**
- **Avoid tokenism.**

Local consultation

- **Quality Protects** One objective of the Quality Protects framework is actively to involve children and families in planning and reviewing the services they need and to show that families are becoming more satisfied with services. Agencies need to consider what policies and structures they have in place to achieve this, both at a strategic level (user consultation and involvement in planning service development) and at an individual and family level (e.g. planning meetings and reviews).
- **PALS** The objectives of the NHS Patient and Liaison Service are to involve and consult with patients and public in decision-making about health care.

The PALS website
www.doh.gov.uk/patientadvice andliaisonservices

MAKING IT WORK

Service providers, whether statutory or voluntary, need to consider how they will consult effectively with users, both the person cared for and the children and young people, in order to inform development of services.

Young carers exist within a set of personal circumstances and relationships where other family members also have needs and the right to be consulted about how services are developed.

"Involving disabled parents and their national and regional organisation in policy development and service monitoring is essential if services are to be developed which disabled parents find welcoming and supportive."
(Wates, 2002)

Good practice example: The Young Carers' Strategy for West Sussex

The Young Carers Strategy for West Sussex is built on consultation with families, young carers groups and professionals.

The messages from families and young carers were presented to groups of multi-agency professionals, disabled parents and carers. These messages reflected the professionals' experiences and positive feedback was received – they felt they had learnt from the consultation and would consider the issues in day-to-day practice.

The messages also informed the content of West Sussex Strategy. Young carers designed posters to accompany a strategy to raise awareness of their stress to professionals and make other young carers aware of the availability of support.

Consultation with young carers in West Sussex is ongoing. Recently a group of young carers met with County Council members and further meetings are planned. Young carers have taken an active role in the Best Value Review (Sub-review for Young Carers). One young carer holds a 'Portfolio for Young Carers' with the county's Youth Cabinet. Her role is to ensure the needs and views of young carers are represented to the Youth Cabinet, regarding both caring and non-caring issues. Some of the young carers in the county are now planning a video project to raise awareness of the issues affecting their lives. They wish to target this at professionals, particularly teachers.

MAKING IT WORK

Children and young people should be consulted and offered real opportunities to participate in shaping practice provision and policies.

Making decisions and choices

> *"We need social workers to listen to our needs and our views and not make up their minds what we want."*
>
> (Young carer)

Enabling young carers and their families to become more involved in the planning processes will enable them to make better decisions and choices and should result in more effective use of resources. It can also give children 'permission' to make choices about their lives.

> *"I would like them [agencies] to learn more from talking to our family."*

> *"It is very important to feel that we can trust the social worker who comes into our home. We don't like be asked to go upstairs or not included in the conversations if we are involved in helping to care for someone in family."*

Many young carers' projects act as advocates and enable children and their families to access information in order to make decisions and informed choices.

Family Group Conferences

Some local authorities use Family Group Conferences (FGC) to help families make decisions about the services that they need. The FGC model can also bridge the gaps between adults' and children's services and involve all the agencies that need to support the whole family. A pilot piece of work was undertaken in Hampshire by The Children's Society to evaluate use of FGCs in families where some had care needs and a child was caring (see Lupton, 2000).

> "Family group conferences can look at the needs of the young carer and any parenting support needs in the context of the wider family and would take account of the whole kin network in the way that other service approaches do not."
>
> (Nixon, *Child Care in Practice* (NI) vol. 5 1999)

> *"Recognise that our family is probably the 'expert' on the situation and work towards what our family wants."*
>
> (Young carer quoted in The Children's Society, 2000)

2. The need for coherent inter-agency strategies and policies

"After my friend had a young carer's assessment from children's services, her worker discussed it with adult services. They could then see why it was important to put some home care in to help all the family."

(From: Underdown, A. 'I'm Growing Up Too Fast' in *Children and Policy Journal*, Vol. 16 No. 1 (2002) pp. 57–60)

Inter-agency strategies and policies have been developed in some areas and are in the planning process in others. Some, but not all, Health Authorities have ensured that the needs of young carers are mentioned in Health Improvement Plans (Corlyn, 2001). When planning services, it is important to recognise both the value of the support offered by young carers' projects and also the need to develop support in mainstream services.

MAKING IT WORK

Agencies need to consider how they will work together to provide coherent and equitable support and services to young carers and those for whom they care.

Good practice example: Quality Protects

In 2000 a number of young carers' projects in the north-west of England and the Regional Quality Protects Coordinator undertook a survey identifying issues for young carer services. This highlighted the need for more uniformity in the kind of help and support that young carers and their families can expect across local boundaries. There were many examples of good practice, but some services suffered from being vulnerable, inconsistent, uncoordinated and uncertain on safeguarding issues.

A number of recommendations were made, including clear eligibility criteria and related policies, visibility in strategic plans, multi-agency policy and procedures and a consistent assessment framework. The overall challenge was to gain commitment to a Regional Action Plan.

The *Regional Quality Protects Forum* supported and gave its commitment to developing and implementing these recommendations. In response to this, a Young Carers' Work Forum was created. Between autumn 2001 and spring 2002 this Forum worked on creating a common definition of 'young carer', together with minimum standards for assessment and service provision. The standards have been devised for both mainstream services as well as for specific services and projects for young carers. This draft document was completed and endorsed by the Regional Quality Protects Forum. It is intended that the final document will be available by the end of 2002.

(Source: Sandra Bilsborrow, North West Young Carers' Work Forum)

MAKING IT WORK

Supporting families who have complex needs is challenging and workers need to have clarity around boundaries of responsibility, where there may be conflicts of interest, whilst still thinking holistically.

Good practice examples

Both Hampshire and Worcestershire Local Authorities have inter-agency strategies and policies in place:

Worcestershire

Worcestershire's objectives include:

- awareness-raising at all levels and multi-agency training;
- encouraging GPs to 'tag' young carers' records;
- ensuring social services staff have access to policies and procedures for assessing young carers;
- establishing a working partnership between young carers' project and youth service;
- improving links between schools and health regarding young carers' issues;
- developing support groups across the county.

Hampshire

Hampshire's inter-agency strategy was planned and written jointly by commissioning team members from health, education and social services working in partnership with the voluntary sector. It also includes acknowledgement of the views of young carers. A set of objectives and measurable standards was written for those working with young carers to implement:

- To enable a young carer to be a child first and foremost as reflected in the UN Convention on the Rights of the Child.
- To work in a holistic way to meet the complex needs of young carers and to help maintain family stability.
- To be aware of and respond to individual needs of young carers.
- To ensure that staff, practitioners and volunteers are given inter-agency support and training.
- To minimise any impact that caring may have on a child's physical, emotional and educational development.
- To ensure effective working between agencies and between providers of services for adults and children.

From: *Taking Responsibility: Hampshire County Council inter-agency policy supporting young carers* (revised 2002)

MAKING IT WORK

Offer all practitioners access to inter-agency training and support.

Good practice examples

North Yorkshire and York

North Yorkshire and York have produced guidelines for staff, which include the following points:

- Ensure there is a senior manager responsible for young carer issues.
- Provide clear information on rights in formats and locations suitable for young people.
- Recognise there are likely to be complex family dynamics which will require sensitive handling.
- Keep up to date on issues and local and national developments.

Lowestoft NHS Primary Care Trust

Lowestoft NHS Primary Care Trust conducted some research on the needs of young carers and their families which informed a report published in 2001 and multi-agency working, service models and health improvement plans.

The need for emotional support and understanding

"We're working blindly, trying to deal with our feelings, feeling guilty for relying on our children. You know they're not responsible for you but they feel they are. You know they're angry and there's nowhere for them to go to before it develops. The anger festers until it gets too much and it explodes. You can hear the desperation with professionals that they haven't got the resources, but they're so defensive. The door closes against you and you will never go and knock again. My doctor said to my child 'Look after mummy, you're the healthiest one in the family.' We need more than recognition. We need understanding. Everyone always asks how I am. Ask about my child."

(West Sussex Disabled Parents and Carers, November 2001)

Someone to talk to – someone to listen

> *"We only talk to people we trust, I never talked to anyone until I went to the Project."*

Young carers say that one of their key needs is emotional support and someone to talk to. This is still vital for them, even if adequate services are being given to the person in need of care.

> *"Even if 24 hour care is provided, we are still young people who care. Feelings, emotions and insecurities about parents, brothers and sisters do not disappear."*
> (Young carer quoted in The Children's Society, 2000)

Young carers say that it can be difficult to share worries with parents and other family members, because they feel they have enough worries of their own. Some families just find it too difficult to acknowledge the illness by talking about it openly and may need support in coming to terms with both the illness and the changes it brings to family life.

> *"I can't talk to mum about things, she gets too upset."*
> (Young carer)

> *"I don't like to try and explain things to him in case it upsets him."*
> (Parent)

Young carers' projects provide emotional support at a range of levels: a chance to talk to a worker, peer support, one-to-one befriending, or arranging for counselling provision, if needed. (See Chapter 7 for further discussion of specific services offered by projects.)

Time and again, young carers say they gain a great deal of emotional support simply by knowing they have someone to talk to. They benefit from talking not only to project workers, but also to each other.

> *"It's good to talk to others in the same position."*

> *"They [project workers] understand how I feel."*

This is also appreciated by the parents of the young carers:

> *"We value the support our son gets from the project."*

> *"It helps me to know that if he doesn't want to talk over something with me he has a place to go and someone who understands the issues should he want to discuss them."*

MAKING IT WORK

It is important to recognise that children may need help and support before the parent is ready to accept their level of care needs and recognise the impact on their children. There must be an accessible gateway to services for such children.

Listening to and supporting the person who needs care is also important to the family and young carer.

> *"I think it was the first time I met [project worker]...She sort of sat us down and asked us what and she let us ramble on for ages, she wrote everything down. That is the first time I think we thought that we might actually get out of our hole."*
> (Shah and Hatton, 1999)

> *"[The development worker] is great, especially when my mum is down... She supports the whole family; mum sometimes rings her up just to talk to her. She listens to both my mum and my dad, especially my mum when she is down. So I know when I need help, I can just call on the project."*

3. The need for effective, sensitive, timely and flexible support

As outlined above, provision of support and services needs to be a multi-agency responsibility and be delivered holistically. The majority of young carers' projects are currently located in the voluntary sector but work in partnership with statutory agencies who provide services to the person with care needs if they meet eligibility criteria.

Young carers in Black communities

It is essential that the multi-agency support that is required to meet the needs of young carers and their families comprehensively embraces the needs of those in Black communities and other cultures. A report by the Greater Manchester Black Young Carers Working Group (Carers National Association, 1996) recommended that:

- **support for Black young carers must be permanent and an integral part of mainstream provision;**
- **service provision needs to be proactive with regards to addressing racism.**

Shah and Hatton (1999) recommend that services should be culturally sensitive, anti-racist and avoid cultural stereotyping.

The National Black Carers Workers Network, in association with The Afiya Trust, have produced *We Care Too: A good practice guide for people working with Black carers* (Powell, E. et al., 2002). Written by frontline workers in the care field, it is the first of its kind to capture the realities of caring as experienced by Black carers, with the aim of improving recognition, services and support to Black carers. The guide provides comprehensive and detailed research into every facet of caring, and endeavours to give effective and practical solutions to concerns expressed by Black people.

It offers the following recommendations:

- **Young carers' lives should be understood from their cultural perspective.**
- **Professionals need to undertake a holistic approach to assessment, which engages families in the process, while acknowledging the need to work from an anti-racist perspective.**
- **Young Black carers should be offered a safe place to have access to people with whom they can readily identify. Many young carers are reluctant to expose their home situation to social/health care workers for fear of being taken into care.**
- **The need for professional interpreters should be properly addressed.**
- **There is a need for the development of a joint-agency approach involving health, social services, education and employment services as well as relevant Black organisations. Their aim should be to offer young Black carers and their families real and lasting opportunities. This could serve to reduce or eliminate their exclusion.**
- **Young Black carers should be involved strategically in an advisory capacity, including full consultation in local authority equality strategies. This will begin to break down some of the barriers to services, which they and their families face currently.**

Good practice example: Oldham Young Carers' Project

Oldham Young Carers' Project includes young Black carers on the Project's multi-disciplinary advisory group. Strategies were developed within the community, via schools and Black organisations, to assist in the identification of young Black carers in order to provide appropriate and relevant support.

Services for parents who have care needs

- Parents who are disabled or ill need to have timely, sensitively written information telling them about the illness or disability and its implications. They need to know about the range of services available to them to support their care needs, and any parenting needs.
- They need to know how to access an assessment and be given information on the roles and responsibilities of key agencies (see Chapter 3).
- Early intervention and support through flexible care packages may prevent children from undertaking inappropriate physical or emotional care.
- Agencies need to develop strategies and practice to meet the needs of episodic illness and those families who do not meet the threshold of eligibility criteria for services but whose children are undertaking, or are likely to undertake, inappropriate care tasks.

"Recognise the importance of involving parents in developing and evaluating assessments and services."
(Wates, 2002)

MAKING IT WORK

When a parent has a sensory impairment, ensure that services consider the specific communication needs of these families so that children are not left to deal inappropriately with correspondence or telephone conversations regarding the health needs of the family member.

Resources

Disabled Parents Network (DPN)

Disabled Parents Network (DPN) is a national pan-disability organisation of disabled people who are parents, or who hope to become parents. Its aims are to provide information, support and advice and to bring about change, which will enable disabled parents to take part in society on an equal basis with non-disabled parents.

DPN has a Disabled Support Worker who provides information, advocacy and ongoing support to disabled parents by speaking to social workers, solicitors, visiting families and supporting them during case conferences or assessments of need.

The Disabled Parents Network website: **www.disabledparentsnetwork.org.uk**

The Royal Association for Disability and Rehabilitation (RADAR)

The Royal Association for Disability and Rehabilitation is a national organisation of and for disabled people. Its key areas of activity are:

- supporting over 500 local and national disability organisations;
- campaigning for improvements in disabled people's lives;
- providing information to support independence and equality for disabled people.

The Royal Association for Disability and Rehabilitation website: **www.radar.org.uk**

Services for families who have children who are disabled or unwell

In common with parents who themselves have care needs (see above), parent carers need timely information about their child's condition, information on how to access an assessment of need, and information on the range of services available to support their child and themselves in their caring role. The assessment should recognise and monitor any needs of siblings and if required ensure the service package to the family takes account of any identified needs.

Resources

MENCAP is able to offer specific support and advice to families where a member has a learning disability, as is National Development Team (NDT) – a national organisation working with people with learning disabilities.

MENCAP website:
www.mencap.org.uk

NDT website:
www.ndt.org.uk

Services for young carers

> *"The time I need help most is when they get home from school, teatime, bathtime and bedtime. It doesn't happen."*
> (Parent care receiver)

> *"Someone to sit with mum at night time would mean I could get some sleep."*
> (Young carer)

Children's needs vary and each family situation will be different. While some children will just need 'someone to talk to', others who have been undertaking an inappropriate level of care may need a complete range of services and support from a number of agencies according to their assessed needs.

MAKING IT WORK

Services supporting young carers need to promote their health and well-being and be responsive to individual needs.

Services that young carers and their families value will be:

- **integrated into the family's own support networks, taking into account the contribution of the child/other family carers to personal/household care tasks;**
- **coordinated between different agencies and across district/divisional boundaries (so services follow if family moves);**

- culturally appropriate, sensitive and responsive, including appropriate match of user and helper;
- sustainable/secure over time (e.g. continuing health care for chronic illness);
- flexible, responding to changing circumstances/conditions, fluctuation, deterioration, improvement;
- timely, sufficient, consistent and secure to prevent crisis/breakdown – a preventive approach to service provision, including simple, practical things at an early stage, before crisis point;
- available without a battle.

From: Department of Health (1996b)

MAKING IT WORK

Agencies need to consider how services can:

- be provided more flexibly and faster
- meet changing or episodic conditions
- include plans for crisis provision.

CHAPTER 5
Supporting Young Carers in School

"Every school will have young carers... and just one individual teacher or support worker being involved can make a huge difference."
(Northamptonshire Young Carers Service, PRTC, 2001)

Introduction

For many children with caring responsibilities, school is the one place that can offer them normality. Teachers, more than many other professionals, have day-to-day contact with young carers, and so it seems appropriate for this guide to devote a major section to the issue of young carers at school.

Although, understandably, teachers see themselves primarily as educators, there are a number of ways in which they can support young carers without compromising this role. More importantly, the support and understanding given by teachers will help young carers reach their full educational potential.

> *"We spend most of our time at home or in school, so it's vital that schools recognise and understand our needs, wants and aspirations."*
> (The Children's Society, 2001)

> *"I need school to understand how hard it is and why our homework is late and why we are tired after Mum has been on a bender."*
> (Young carer)

This chapter offers guidance to schools on practical ways in which they can help young carers and their families, including:

- ways of identifying young carers;
- ways of encouraging young carers and their parents to feel they can approach the school and ask for help;
- promoting positive images of disability;
- PHSE and Citizenship curriculum guidance;
- how to tackle some of the major issues within the school environment that young carers see as being priorities, including bullying, pupil support;

- young carers in need of extra educational support;
- young carers and school exclusions;
- creating a school policy on working with young carers;
- staff training;
- working with other support agencies.

The final section of this chapter discusses the issues faced by young carers who are aged 16 and over, and who are therefore making choices about further education, careers and leaving home.

The effects of caring responsibilities on a young person's education

> *"Young carers often make enormous efforts to manage their caring responsibilities and maintain full school attendance. However, some may struggle to cope all the time and subsequently their education, physical and mental health may be affected. Young carers can often feel as if they have somehow failed or feel extremely guilty for not coping."*
> (Baker, 2002)

The Young Carers Research Group at University of Loughborough undertook a study of 650 young carers in 1998 and found that:

- 86% were of school age;
- 1 in 5 young carers missed school because of caring responsibilities;
- 28% of young carers aged 5–15 were experiencing educational difficulties;
- 1 in 3 young carers at secondary school were experiencing educational difficulties.

Further research by The Princess Royal Trust for Carers (1999) revealed that 71% of the young carers questioned had experienced bullying at school.

The research group at Loughborough University also examined the experiences of young people aged 16–25 who had been caring as a child. They found the following:

- A large proportion had educational problems and had missed school. Many had failed to attain educational qualifications. This, combined with ongoing caring responsibilities, meant that some young carers were excluded from the labour market.
- Half the sample had missed school and a quarter had no GCSEs.

Career and job choice were sometimes influenced by the skills gained through caring (Dearden and Becker, 2000).

Two other reports revealed similar findings: *On Small Shoulders* (The Children's Society, 1999) looked at the experiences of former young carers and found that the education of many young carers is easily disrupted and that caring frequently has an impact on future life chances and career choices. *Caring Alone: Young carers in South Asian communities* (Shah and Hatton, 1999) also found that most young carers who took part in the study reported experiencing problems with educational achievement as a consequence of caring.

> *"I want to achieve; I want to do well... I do try hard but nobody seems to realise what's going on at home. They [the teachers] say, 'You're not doing your best...' But it is my best."*
>
> (Young carer quoted in Frank, 1995)

MAKING IT WORK

Ensure that young carers have the same access to a full education and career choices as their peers.

Case study

The following is taken from a quote by a young woman aged 16, originally published in Bibby and Becker (2000).

"I had to leave school in February because I was having a lot of time off to look after my mum. I missed out on a lot of coursework, which had to be in before my exams. It wasn't worth it because I'd only been entered for two exams. So I left school to just look after my mum. I've been doing it since nine. Housework, washing, washing-up, used to have to wash my mum as well. Just something I ended up doing. I do the decorating all through the house, front and back garden, cleaning the kitchen, everything, bedrooms, bathroom, I have to do it all. We used to have someone to come in to do the living room, but then you had to pay for it. We couldn't afford it so we stopped it.

She needs someone to prepare her dinner. I do it, normally.

She couldn't be here on her own. I used to phone up from school but sometimes she couldn't hear the phone and I used to get worried. I used to walk out of school to come home to make sure she was all right. They used to think I was making it up – as an excuse for not being in school.

Education welfare just say, 'It's no excuse for her to be off school, you need to get help in'. But it's easier said than done. Having the money problems that we had, it's quite expensive now to have a carer in.

If my mum never had the stroke I'd probably still be in school. All my coursework would have been in, I would have been able to concentrate on just one thing – on school – and then, perhaps, I would have gone to college. Perhaps I would have just gone straight into work, I'll never know now."

Identifying a young carer in school

> *"They need to recognise the signs that someone needs help and be there to listen."*
> (Young carer)

An added difficulty for schools is that children often do not want or feel able to confide that they are caring and that they need extra help and consideration. They may not want to appear to be different or may not be aware that they can ask for help. They may be embarrassed about their home situation, particularly if they are caring for someone with alcohol dependency, substance misuse, mental ill health or a learning disability. They may wish to forget about responsibilities and see school as an escape. They may fear teasing or bullying and have a fear of interference or change that may result in the family being split up.

Equally, as discussed in Chapter 1, many children do not identify themselves as young carers or recognise the impact that caring is having upon them until a crisis is reached. This makes the task for schools a daunting one. But it is nevertheless extremely important.

> *"It was when I happened to fall asleep in class that they found out my mum was ill...I didn't used to talk to anyone. I suppose that was my own fault but then, I didn't know anyone was interested."*
> (Young carer quoted in Clark, 1996)

The impact of the family situation on a young person at home will vary from pupil to pupil but the points listed below show some common examples of signs that may indicate if a child is undertaking inappropriate levels of care:

Signs that may indicate that a child is caring for someone at home

- **Arriving late at school**
- **Unable to complete homework on time**
- **Difficulty concentrating in class**
- **Behavioural dificulties**
- **Missing school**
- **Tired**
- **Withdrawn, over-sensitive**
- **Clothing or appearance may not be clean or tidy**
- **Low self-esteem**
- **Under-achieving**

MAKING IT WORK

Ensure that the school provides ways of encouraging young carers and their parents to feel they can approach the school and ask for help if needed.

- **Ill health (e.g. stress-related illnesses, back problems from lifting, anxiety, depression)**
- **Difficulties in mixing with peers and joining in after-school activities and in attending school trips (e.g. residential)**
- **Being bullied**
- **Some parents are unable to have contact with school – missing parents evenings, for example**
- **Financial difficulties**

(Source: Northamptonshire Young Carers Service PRTC, 2001)

"Yawning gets you into trouble – they say you should go to bed earlier – they won't let you explain you've been up all night."

(West Sussex Young Carers' Strategy)

Using PSHE sessions and assemblies

The first step to enabling pupils to identify themselves as young carers can be through presentations in assemblies, Personal, Social and Health Education (PSHE) sessions and by displaying information on school notice boards about support offered by the school for young carers.

There is a range of materials available that is suitable for both primary and secondary pupils on the issues of caring in the community and young carers. There is also a wide choice of materials that address disability, mental ill health and alcohol and substance misuse. A list can be found on pages 88–89.

All materials include a section on planning and delivery. However, the following general points need to be considered when planning and giving lessons:

- **Establish some ground rules to provide a safe working environment.**
- **Have a plan in place to deal with any young carer who may self-identify and ask for help during or following the lesson.**
- **Be sensitive about case studies/materials used, which may reflect the reality of a pupil in the group.**
- **Ensure that the materials used include a named person, helplines or contact numbers in case a child wants to ask for help following the lesson.**

Consider how disability, illness and caring issues can be incorporated into other lessons such as Drama, Humanities, Religious Education and Citizenship.

Admissions forms

Schools could include a statement on the admissions form to help identify families where someone has a long-term illness or care needs. (For example, 'please inform the school if there are any other family circumstances which you feel the school should be aware of: e.g. disability/ill health'.)

Home-school agreement

The home-school agreement could be amended to include a question asking if any extra support is needed or if there is any illness/disability in the family which may impact on the child/parents keeping to the agreement.

> *"My mum can't visit school... It's too far to walk and there are too many stairs and corridors."*
> (Young carer)

MAKING IT WORK

Ensure all teaching staff, appropriate support staff e.g. special needs assistants, educational welfare staff and staff in units for education (other than at schools) and governors are given access to awareness-raising sessions and training on educational and pastoral issues for young carers.

The importance of being sensitive

If staff suspect that a child is caring, then an approach needs to be made sensitively. The following quote illustrates just how difficult it is to get it right:

> "I was sitting in a corner and I was crying. The teacher just turned up. He asked me if everything was alright. I said yes but one of my friends must have said to him she's not. She had just said things are difficult and have been for a long time. So he did know something, but after that he didn't ask any more questions. I would have been very resentful if he'd have asked at the time, but maybe if he did things might have been different."
> (Shah and Hatton, 1999)

Provision of support: young carers' views

Dearden and Becker (2000) found that some young people view the practical skills acquired through caring as important and useful for independence and adulthood. The positive aspects of caring do need to be remembered and valued: young carers can be more mature and responsible, gain a range of life skills, and have empathy and tolerance of disability and illness.

Yet, whenever a group of young carers are consulted, their educational needs and the wish for better understanding and support always dominate discussions. At the first Young Carers' Festival (see Chapter 2) young carers told us:

> *"Teachers should be aware of the situation at home."*

> *"Try to find out more about young carers so that teachers understand when children talk about their problems."*

The following pages discuss practical ways in which schools can support young carers.

Young carers say they need:

- information
- positive images of disability
- somewhere to go to talk
- to be accepted and understood
- help if they are being bullied
- confidentiality
- emotional support and understanding
- help with keeping up with work

Information

- Make information regarding health issues and local community services available and accessible to all pupils in school. (This needs to be a dedicated notice board which is updated regularly.)
- Ensure information about any local support for young carers, helplines, etc is accessible to all pupils.
- Schools should include information about disability (including mental health) and young carers in PSHE sessions so that illness and differences are respected and understood.

MAKING IT WORK

Enable pupils to access information independently if they choose, by displaying up-to-date information about support and resources in the community.

Positive images of disability

It is important to promote positive images of disability throughout the school curriculum and the school environment. One example of good practice would be to invite local disability/mental health organisations to be involved in PSHE sessions, or to give a presentation during assembly. In addition to this, also consider:

- ensuring that parents who are disabled or ill feel able to be part of the school community and have equal access to the school – including open evenings, concerts – and are able to communicate with tutors when needed;
- using PSHE and Citizenship sessions to explore how other agencies such as social services, Citizens Advice, Benefits Agency, etc can help communities;
- choosing topics of disability, ill health and caring as an assembly theme and ensuring appropriate resources are available afterwards, including opportunities to talk to someone.

MAKING IT WORK

Promote positive images of disability, illness, mental ill health and caring throughout the school curriculum and environment.

Somewhere to go to talk

Ensure there is an appropriately trained adult in every school who can act on any concerns and provide somewhere private where pupils can go to talk with a staff member if needed. Young people also need to be reassured that confidentiality will be respected.

> *"It's difficult to talk to the teachers. It's not easy to explain... It's always in the corridor or class. I just don't tell them."*
> (Young carer quoted in Frank, 1995)

> *"It's important knowing you can talk when you need to... but not feeling you have to..."*
> (Young carer quoted in Shah and Hatton, 1999)

> *"Today at school I told my teacher I was worried. She asked me why, I told her nothing. I felt so worried. Sometimes you feel angry at the person you care for, which makes you feel selfish and you know you shouldn't. It's time consuming and tough. I'm always thinking about how she's doing and it takes my mind off school. How am I supposed to explain myself? I help my mum feel better, and that makes me feel good."*
> (Young carer quoted in Shah and Hatton, 1999)

To be accepted and understood

Children often say that they are stigmatised at school. They say they feel isolated or that they are seen as problem children if they are unable to complete homework tasks or are repeatedly late or absent.

> *"Teachers need to know that many children are young carers and they need to understand our family situations, what we have to do and how we feel."*
> (The Children's Society, 2000)

Help if they are bullied

Many young carers say they are bullied at school. In their report on this issue, Crabtree and Warner (1999) gave a number of reasons for this:

Young carers may:

- have greater maturity than (and so may not be accepted by) peers;
- have minimal social skills;
- find it harder to make and sustain friendships;
- be withdrawn;
- be over-sensitive;

- have untidy or unclean clothing or general appearance;
- be teased or ostracised because of family circumstances.

> *"People call me names and laugh at my family at school."*
> (Young carer)

The report recommends that school bullying policies should refer to the specific needs of young carers who are being bullied.

MAKING IT WORK

Have policies and practice in place to prevent bullying, stigmatisation and to raise the self-esteem of children who are young carers.

Confidentiality

The following are important points to bear in mind when talking to young carers:

- Be sensitive and do not discuss young carers' situations in front of other pupils or parents.
- Respect a child's views.
- Be aware that young carers may be embarrassed at the idea of sharing details of their home situation with their teacher.
- Some may have feelings of disloyalty and so be anxious about talking.
- Others will fear that the family may be split up or that they have failed if they need to ask for help.

An accepting environment

> *"They should find different ways of communicating with parents, e.g. tape for blind parent."*
> (Young Carers' Festival, Voice 2000)

> *"My tutor comes to visit mum and me. It helps a lot."*
> (Young carer)

Many young carers do not realise that help may be available for them or for the person in need of care and may keep coping until they reach a crisis point. A school that is 'disability-friendly', open about mental ill health and people who need care will provide an environment where young carers feel able to speak to someone if they need help.

Be aware that parents may find it emotionally very difficult to talk to staff about their illness and their own needs and those of their children. A home visit to talk may be a helpful approach for some families.

> *"I have a card I can show to my teacher if I am upset in class. She will always find time to talk to me."*
> (The Children's Society, 2000)

> *"The headmaster lets my mum park in the staff car park."*
> (Young carer)

Emotional support and understanding

"We would like teachers to communicate more effectively with each other so that everyone who teaches us understands if we are late, absent or need extra support or time for homework."
(The Children's Society, 2000)

"We need to be able to feel that we can talk to someone who will listen and understand and treat information in a confidential manner."
(The Children's Society, 2000)

- Respond sensitively to young carers' needs and be sensitive to the needs of all family members.
- Take time to identify why a child is absent, late for school or exhibiting disruptive behaviour before considering disciplinary action.

"When my mother became ill, I was about 14, I became the class trouble maker... which was quite unusual because I was always a goody goody up until then."
(Former carer quoted in Frank, Tatum and Tucker, 1999)

"Give us more support when we are upset."
(Young Carers' Festival, Voice 2000)

"Understand if we ever feel down."
(Young Carers Festival, Voice 2000)

"Don't forget, boys care too. And remember sibling carers!"
(The Children's Society, 2000)

"The school counsellor is a great help."
(Young carer)

Help with keeping up with work

"I miss school quite a bit sometimes. I can't leave my mum on her own, 'cos like sometimes in the morning sometimes she's really, really scared to be at home by herself."
(Munoz, 1998)

- Consider how to provide extra support to help young carers achieve their full potential, including any assessment of special needs that they might have.

"I used to do my homework at about 4 o'clock in the morning. Even now I wake up at 4 in the morning."
(Former carer quoted in Frank, Tatum and Tucker, 1999)

Consider provision to deliver missed education before a pupil completely drops out of school or crises develop. Types of provision that young carers say would help include:

- lesson notes for missed classes;
- identified time with staff for catching up/extra help;
- support from special educational needs (if educational attainment is affected);
- lunchtime homework clubs;
- flexibility with workloads and coursework deadlines.

If needed, consider (with pupil's consent) notifying exam boards of any barriers to revising or completing coursework.

> *"Before, they didn't really know what was going on. But then my grades started to drop a bit, and they were worried so they talked to my social worker and then she explained the situation and then they were giving me extra help to get my grades back up and everything."*
> (Munoz, 1998)

> *"My teachers are understanding. They give me extra time for homework."*
> (Young carer, Canterbury)

MAKING IT WORK

Many young carers' projects work with schools and help establish lunchtime clubs, drop-in sessions and other support as needed.

Examples of good practice:

Norwich and District Carers Forum – Young Carers' Schools Project is one project that has excellent links with schools and other agencies. Its aims are to identify and give support to young carers in high schools in East, North, Central and South Norfolk. Services offered include support groups, training for professionals, awareness-raising lessons and assemblies in schools.

Other projects offering services to schools include: Lewisham Carers PRTC, Kettering PRTC, Brent Young Carers' Project, Hillingdon Young Carers' Project PRTC.

Other practical suggestions that work for young carers

- Access to a telephone helps to give peace of mind about the situation at home. This may help pupils concentrate in lesson time and feel supported by the school. Some schools provide special phone passes.
- Young carers identity card: *"So we don't have to explain all the time – so we can get an early lunch and then go and do our homework."*
- A buddy system.

- Consider developing drop-in support sessions that enable young carers to feel safe about talking to someone if they need to. This could be specifically aimed at young carers or be part of existing drop-in facilities.

> *"Have somewhere for us to go and meet other people in school who are in the same boat."*
> (Young Carers' Festival, Voice 2000)

- Consider other forms of discipline rather than after-school detentions.

> *"Don't give us after-school detentions because we have to look after people at home or collect younger brothers and sisters."*
> (The Children's Society, 2000)

- Use school newsletters to raise awareness of the school's disability policy and support offered for young carers.
- Make links with school nurses. (For example, Southampton Young Carers has a group that meets at a secondary school and is run by the school nurse.)

Exclusion policy

Research and practice has shown that some young carers are given temporary or permanent exclusions. This may happen because the school is unaware of the home situation and sees only the behaviour issues. Only after the exclusion has been implemented may the real situation become apparent.

The **Pupil Support Social Inclusion Statement** (see page 83) offers guidance to schools on encouraging inclusion for young carers.

Schools' exclusion policies and any initiatives to reduce school exclusion and introduce pupil support plans should include awareness of young carer issues.

> "Particular regard needs to be given to supporting children from ethnic groups who are more likely to be excluded from school."
> (Department of Health, 1999c)

Evaluating Educational Inclusion (OFSTED, 2000) includes young carers in the list of different groups for which schools need to identify, collect and record performance data, and have strategies for support to raise standards.

Educational support

Local Education Authority and agency policies (e.g. Education Welfare Officers, Educational Psychology, Education Other Than At School (EOTAS), Youth and Career services) should also include provision for young carers and have an inter-agency strategy to support them.

Recommendations to Education Welfare Officers for getting young carers back on track

- If a young person is routinely absent from school, consideration must be given to the health status of a relative at home to whom that young person may be providing care.
- Young carers may feel anxious to go to school and guilty about leaving the person they care for, because of their care needs. Childcare responsibilities for young siblings and/or the absence of assistance to the parent in transporting their child to school must also be taken into account when working with young carers who are frequent absentees.
- Consider providing home tutoring to pupils who are clearly unable to attend school as a result of their caring responsibilities.
- Ask the parent(s) what support and/or services they would like to access, to enable their child to return to school and to help ease the level of care given by their child to a relative at home. The longer a child is absent from school, the more anxious they may feel in returning to school because of the concept they have as to how far behind they may be with their studies in comparison to their peers.
- Ask the child what support they would like to receive from their school that may help them feel more confident in returning to school. Remember to ask if the child would feel less anxious leaving the person for whom they cared, if they were given access to a telephone during the school day. Also ask the parent(s) and child if they can identify a teacher who can be given details of their caring responsibilities at home.
- Liaise with the young carer's school, and ensure that the school has simple policies in place for supporting young carers returning to school after a period of absence.

(Taken from Baker, 2002)

Working with other agencies

> *"School staff may be the first to be aware of the young caring situation, and therefore be the key to setting the tone for the service response and triggering inter-agency action."*
> (Department of Health, 1996b)

The Carers (Recognition and Services) Act 1995 Policy Guidance and Practice Guide states that social services departments should work closely with local education authorities when carrying out assessments of young carers. Section 166 of the Education Act 1993 also places a qualified duty on social services departments to assist local education authorities in work with children who have special educational needs.

National Healthy Schools Standard Guidance (Department for Education and Employment, 1999a) supports the development of local healthy schools programmes. The standards can be used assist with supporting young carers through the partnerships formed with health and the process of standard setting, monitoring and evaluation.

Website:
www.wiredforhealth.gov.uk

The National Strategy Caring for Carers (Department of Health, 1999c) highlights the need for cross-agency work to support young carers:

- **to ensure that young carers have the same access to opportunities such as education, good health and leisure time;**
- **to ensure effective practice in meeting the needs of pupils who are young carers through links with young carers' projects;**
- **to encourage schools to designate a link officer for young carers, linking them with social services, the health service and young carers' projects;**
- **to use the pupil inclusion guidance when giving support;**
- **to raise awareness of young carers in schools through ensuring that teaching on PSHE includes the issue of young carers;**
- **for schools to be sensitive to the individual problems faced by young carers, such as arriving late or missing school, which can disrupt a child's education.**

When a child is caring for a family member without the appropriate support, it will impact on their school life and their emotional and physical well-being. Once you realise that a pupil is a young carer, it is important to establish the level of care they provide – ie. what they need to do, and why.

Talk to the pupil about his or her own right to an assessment and ask if they would like to be put in touch with a young carers' project or similar support group (see Chapter 3). If an assessment is to be provided in school for the young carer, it is important that the parents know you are aware that their son or daughter may need help, and may need to give some family information.

Arrange to meet with the parents and ask if they are receiving sufficient support and whether there are ways in which the school could assist, such as liaising with other agencies for extra support in the home.

Consider ways of linking and involving external agencies and support to reduce the workload of teaching staff.

Good practice

- Make use of external agencies.
- Use existing partnerships formed through healthy schools standards, schools mentoring services, school nurses, etc.
- Make contact with:
  – local young carers' project,
  – Youth Advisory Service.
- Allocate a member of staff to act as a link between young carers, local projects, Education Welfare and Social Services if needed.
- Have procedures in place for joint working between statutory and voluntary agencies, including counsellors/mentors.
- Include agencies that offer support to the person with care needs.
- If needed, refer pupils to Connexions who have a remit to support young carers. (See below.)
- Ensure links with local bereavement agencies are known in case they are needed. For specific issues (e.g. alcohol dependency) contact relevant voluntary groups. The National Association of Children of Alcoholics (NACOA) has specific guidance to help teachers support children of alcoholics.

MAKING IT WORK

Ensure that an effective working policy is in place to enable inter-agency work to support young carers and their families.

The following information may be useful for teachers who are in contact with young carers. Further details of external support can be found in Chapters 6 and 7.

Connexions

Connexions, the new youth support service for 13- to 19-year-olds, has an important role to play in helping to identify and provide support to young carers. The aim of the service is to ensure that the needs of all young people are recognised and acted upon in order to remove barriers to learning.

Connexions provides a network of personal advisers who will be able to offer advice and support to young carers and put them in touch with appropriate specialist and support services. Priority will be given to those young people who are at risk of not making an easy transition to adulthood. This is done by raising aspirations and removing barriers to their effective engagement with learning.

Solihull Crossroads Young Carers' Project has been successful in developing a strong working partnership with the Birmingham/Solihull Connexions Programme. Through developing a strategic proposal outlining how the key objectives of both the Young Carers' Project and Connexions were parallel, the Solihull Project has secured a seconded Personal Advisor, who will act as a generic Schools Outreach Worker for young carers.

More information about the Connexions Service can be found at their website.

Connexions Service website: **www.connexions.gov.uk**

Learning mentors

Learning mentors are being piloted through the Excellence in Cities initiative to provide one-to-one support for children who are having problems at school (including young carers) and help them access support.

See **www.standards.dfes.gov.uk/excellence/**

More information can also be found at: **www.nmn.org.uk.**

Youth work

Youth work with young carers can provide valuable support for their own personal, social and educational development. Many projects work in partnership with local Youth Service initiatives and some are located within the statutory Youth Service provision.

Counselling

Some young carers may benefit from counselling and this may be provided by a project or be available from school counselling service or other statutory or voluntary provision.

Using school policies and strategies to meet the needs of young carers

National guidance offers structures to schools to help them meet the needs of young carers. The National Strategy for Carers (Department of Health, 1999c) states:

> "All teachers already have duties to promote the general progress and well-being of children, and to provide guidance, as well as advice, to them on educational and social matters. Schools are encouraged to name one member of staff to be the lead for young carers' issues and to link to other agencies as set out in the *Pupil Support Circular.*"

The document *Social Inclusion: Pupil Support Circular* 10/99 (Department for Education and Employment, 1999b) gives this guidance on young carers:

> **3.10 Young carers of a sick or disabled relative at home may be late or absent from school because of their responsibilities. A study in one authority suggested there might be up to 30 young carers in a secondary school.**
>
> **3.11 In a genuine crisis, a school can approve absence for a child to care for a relative until other arrangements can be made. The school should set a time limit for the absence and set some schoolwork so the pupil does not fall far behind while at home. Referral to outside agencies should be done sensitively, recognising that a child may fear being "put into care" if the parents are seen as unable to cope.**
>
> **3.12 Schools should consider designating a member of staff to have responsibility for young carers. They can also contribute to schemes that support them, working with local authorities and voluntary agencies. There may be local schemes to help young carers.**

School can be used to shape and inform practice with young carers and can be used to support staff training.

Policies should refer to the above legislation and also to the school's statutory duties under the 1989 Children Act and consider provision that:

- promotes positive images of disability, mental ill health and caring throughout the school curriculum and environment;
- provides support to any young carers, including a named member of staff with lead responsibility;
- includes issues around disability, mental ill health and young carers in PSHE and Citizenship lessons;
- does not stigmatise or label pupils who are carers and gives guidance on preventing bullying;
- ensures parents can access school for open evenings, etc., and if this is not possible consider how links can be made with home;
- has an agreed confidentiality policy which includes a child protection statement and is adhered to;
- includes thinking about sensitivities and differences around cultural needs, including refugees;
- considers how information on pupils' pastoral needs can be effectively passed between primary and secondary school;
- provides specific staff training;

- includes mechanisms for effective inter-agency work to support young carers (including child protection procedures if required);
- includes mechanisms to consult with young carers and their parents about content of policies and delivery of support;
- includes methods of regularly evaluating effectiveness of policy and support (in addition to meeting OFSTED requirements).

Training

In order to provide genuine and effective support to young carers at school, the following points should be considered:

- Access to awareness-raising sessions and training should be available to all teachers and relevant non-teaching staff.
- Thought should be give to raising awareness with governors. Initially this could happen by involvement in drafting and implementing a policy.
- Be aware that training sessions may raise issues for any staff who were young carers themselves.
- New teachers joining the school need to be remembered and the school policy should also be made available to supply teachers.
- A number of packs have been written to help schools with training in pastoral and PSHE issues and local projects may be able to offer assistance to education authorities and schools. (See pages 88–89.)

MAKING IT WORK

Make links with local young carers' projects who may be able to offer advice, staff support and training.

Linking with local projects

- **Local young carers' projects can often provide training and support to schools.**
- **Invite a project worker to give a presentation at an assembly, but ensure there is a strategy in place for any young carers who may self-identify.**
- **Consider using drama – either pupil-led or done by a professional company – to illustrate disability/mental health and caring issues.**
- **Ensure clarity around:**
  – confidentiality
  – parental consent when speaking to pupils individually or attending specific groups. (A good opportunity to raise awareness by letting parents know in advance of an assembly presentation.)
- **Invite local projects to governor training sessions and pyramid head meetings to raise awareness.**

(Source: Project workers workshops, Reading 2000)

16 plus, careers and leaving home

> *"I would like to go away to university ... but I am worried that as my brother gets older he will be too difficult for my mum to look after."*
> (Young carer)

At the age of 16, young carers may be eligible to claim Invalid Care Allowance, providing they are not studying for more than 21 hours per week. They may also be eligible for financial assistance under the Carers and Disabled Children Act 2000, following an assessment of their own needs as a carer. However, there is no financial assistance available for them or their families to enable them to attend Sixth Form or Further Education (FE) colleges, nor any financial help with transport to college.

Equally, the system of tuition fees and student loans can deter some young carers from applying for university places. Their caring responsibilities mean they are unable to seek part-time employment to help finance their daily living costs at university. If their family is relying on benefits or on a low income, they may feel compelled to seek full-time employment, rather than further education.

> "It may make financial sense for some young people to adopt caring roles in families where they (parent/s) are unable to make adequate financial contributions. This is a 'catch 22' position for many young carers."
> (Dearden and Becker, 2000b)

FE colleges need to be aware of young carers' issues and have policies and practice in place to support them, so that young carers are not disadvantaged and are enabled to have equal opportunities to attend FE courses if they wish. Flexibility and/or support with coursework demands may be needed at times for some young carers.

If a young person has experienced lost opportunities in gaining necessary qualifications, consider how they can be assisted to return to education and have a second chance at obtaining qualifications.

Careers

> "Many young carers have key skills and competencies that go unrecognised and there is currently no way of accrediting such skills... While the acquisition of such will not be best achieved by caring unsupported, such skills, if acknowledged would be an asset to many employers."
> (Dearden and Becker, 2000b)

Frank, Tatum and Tucker (1999) found that many young carers had transferred their caring skills into career/job choice. However, it is important that careers advisors do not assume that this should be the only career path but assist young carers to explore all options.

Young carers can also be highly self-motivated to achieve against all odds.

Action for Carers and Employment (ACE National) is promoting carers' participation in the labour market, including those age 16–18. ACE National will work in seven demonstration sites – Hartlepool, Huddersfield, London, Sunderland, Surrey, Anglesey in North Wales and Carmarthenshire in South Wales – to develop and test mechanisms for supporting carers in and into work. These support mechanisms will then be mainstreamed through ACE National's policy partnership, leaving behind a permanent legacy for carers who want to work.

For more information please contact:
Carers UK,
20/25 Glasshouse Yard,
London EC1A 4JT
Tel: 020 7490 8818
web: carersonline.org.uk

The Connexions service is a good source of advice and support for young carers in this age range. Some young carers' projects are working closely with their local Connexions teams and offering training on young carer issues.

Careers and Connexions services need to consider how they can achieve the following:

- Ensure careers advisors are aware of issues faced by young carers.
- Consider appointing a designated member of the team to build up expertise and knowledge of young carers' issues to share with other colleagues and input to policy.
- Implement the provision of proactive support and advice in career choice.
- Acknowledge and include caring experiences, skills and other strengths gained in young carers' CVs.
- Work towards encouraging employers to recognise the strengths of carers.
- Consider support structures that will assist former young carers to take up 'second chance' educational and vocational opportunities.
- Consider types of support that can be offered if their caring role restricts their going to college or training, particularly if this involves living away from home or travelling a distance.
- Consider part-time courses, distance learning, Open University, community-based short courses, etc.

Working with other agencies

- Develop procedures for communication and referrals between all agencies involved with young carers.
- For those leaving, or likely to leave, education with few qualifications, signpost to the Learning Gateway.

- **Signpost to financial advice (e.g. Citizens Advice Bureau, Benefits Agency).**
- **Develop procedures for communication and referrals between all agencies involved with young carers.**
- **Explore partnership working and joint initiatives.**
- **Keep in contact and monitor progress, by developing an up-to-date and comprehensive register of contacts, with detailed monitoring of progress and outcomes.**
- **Provide an opportunity to respond to shifts in circumstances for a young carer.**

(Sources: Dearden and Becker (2000b) and Surrey Young Carers' Project 'Raising awareness of young carers' issues with the Connexions Training Module, Surrey Young Carers)

Useful websites

Carers (Recognition and Services) Act 1995
www.hmso.gov.uk
National Carers Strategy
www.doh.gov.uk/carers.htm
Evaluating Educational Inclusion OFSTED 2000
www.ofsted.gov.uk
Connexions – the introduction of personal advisors for pupils **www.connexions.gov.uk**
Healthy Schools Standards
www.wiredforhealth.gov.uk
Excellence in Cities
www.standards.dfes.gov.uk/excellence/
Learning Gateway
www.dfes.gov.uk/thelearninggateway/
Mentoring **www.nmn.org.uk**

Resources for use in PHSE sessions

(See also the Bibliography section.)

Young Carers

Baker, G. *Supporting Young Carers in School: A secondary resource pack*. Carers Lewisham, Princess Royal Trust for Carers.

Includes lesson plan ideas and resources.

Carers Together in Hampshire (2001) *Who Cares? Young Carers PSHE Pack: Pupil awareness module for use in schools.*

Includes case studies and worksheets for use in lessons.

Gray, G. *Talking About It: Promoting mental health in schools*. Meridian Broadcasting Charitable Trust.

A pack for use in schools with 11–16-year-olds which includes a section on young carers. Folder of activities, audiotape and video are available.

Northamptonshire Young Carers' Service (2001) *Information Pack for Schools.*

Folder of information, including lesson ideas.

Suffolk County Council (2001) *Understanding Young Carers: A support document for PSE (Key Stage 3, Year 8).*

Includes background information and resources for lessons.

Surrey Young Carers' Project (1998) *Young Carers: Resource pack for schools.*

Includes photocopiable resources and information.

Videos

Cornwall Young Carers' Project (2001) *Who Cares?*

Booklet and video for use by teachers and youth workers.

Hammersmith and Fulham Young Carers *What About Me?*

This video was put together by young people who have a caring role in their family. They express their views about being young carers.

Alcohol

NACOA produces a poster and leaflet for schools, together with additional information supplied to children of alcoholics and professionals working with them.

Disability and illness

The Child Brain Injury Trust has produced a 15-minute video on brain injury and its impact on education, which may be useful in schools.

They are also in the process of updating their education-related information.

NB: They focus on acquired brain injury, which encompasses meningitis, strokes, tumours, etc.

Autism

The National Autism Society have some information on autism for young people, although not necessarily directed at young carers. Some of it is aimed at young people with a classmate with autism and some is for children who have a sibling with autism.

Disability

Saunders, K. (2000) *Happy Ever Afters: A storybook guide to teaching children about disability.* Trentham Books

Mental Health

Young Minds produces a number of booklets for young people. One of the booklets is called 'mental illness in your family' and is written with young carers in mind.

CHAPTER 6
Services for Particular Circumstances

Introduction

This section gives practice guidance for those working with young carers and their families in particular circumstances that may require specific types of support, namely: those helping to care for a sibling; families living in rural areas; families where there is a parent with mental ill health; refugees; families where there is drug misuse or alcohol dependency; families dealing with HIV/AIDs; coping with loss and bereavement. Each of these could form a book in itself, but it is hoped that this chapter will give practitioners food for thought, examples of good practice and pointers towards other resources and sources of expertise.

Support for children helping to care for a brother or sister

Some young carers' projects include sibling carers in their main group. Others have established specific group support for siblings.

Good practice case study: Southampton

The Southampton Sibling Group provides an opportunity for siblings to express some of their feelings of what it is like to grow up with a disabled sibling. Group work helps to combat feelings of isolation and secrecy. It provides siblings with fun activities and a positive experience and a chance to mix with a peer group who have similar experiences to themselves.

The reason behind setting up the group was that there appeared to be a gap in services provided in Southampton for the brothers and sisters of disabled children. These children were not identified as a 'special needs group' and unless their problems reached a severe degree and were referred to Child and Family Guidance, there was no outlet for them to express themselves. The need for the group was identified by workers, parents and the children themselves. It was felt that children should have an opportunity to talk about some

continued overleaf

of the issues that they find difficult to discuss at home. Research carried out locally confirmed that there was a need for such a service in Southampton.

Aims of the group

a) To provide a safe environment where feelings and issues concerning the group members' family situations can be expressed and discussed, and to encourage the children to share both positive and negative feelings about living with disability.

b) To give the young people time and space for themselves away from their families.

c) To provide fun activities and to provide a general positive experience.

Other good practice

Aberdeen Young Carers have a sibling group and Northampton Young Carers have organised a series of sibling activity days in partnership with the Community Team for Learning Disability.

"It's nice to make friends who are in the same position as me. I enjoy the trips as I cannot go out to places because of my brother."

Resources for sibling groups

Contact a Family is a UK charity that helps families who care for children with any disability or special need. It is also a source of information about rare disorders. The Contact a Family Directory Online contains details of many medical conditions and also patient support groups. The information in it is also provided as part of the NHS Direct Online service.

Contact a Family Helpline on 0808 808 3555. Freephone for parents and families (10am–4pm, Mon.–Fri.)
Email: info@cafamily.org.uk
Website: www.cafamily.org.uk

MAKING IT WORK

Remember that not all children who have a brother or sister who is ill or disabled will be undertaking caring responsibilities, but they may have needs that should be considered at times of assessments and reviews.

Young carers in rural areas

Populations in rural areas tend to be relatively scattered and it can therefore be difficult and more expensive to deliver services and carry out home assessments and visits. Grant assistance from central funds reflects population size rather than demography. Families will find it harder to access services, day centres, GPs, hospitals and clinics. This will be further compounded if the family does not have a car or the transport network is poor or unreliable. The inaccessibility of resources and support can compound the needs of young carers. It can also affect their access to recreation, leisure opportunities and socialising.

Young carers' projects who work in rural areas find that transporting the young people to and from group sessions can be time-consuming and expensive. Considerable planning of staffing and resources needs to be done before any activities can be undertaken. Funding for these projects therefore needs to take into account these extra costs in staff time and transport.

MAKING IT WORK

Ensure assessments for the person in need of care consider access to support and services from rural location, if required.

Rural young carers' projects have been established in many areas, including Cornwall, Hampshire, Shropshire, Norfolk, Wales and Scotland.

The Forum for Rural Children and Young People is an umbrella organisation of national bodies seeking to improve the outcomes for children and young people living in rural areas. It plays a key role in exchanging information, sharing good practice and assisting in policy development.

The aim is to bring together a wide range of organisations in order to:

- ensure that the voices of rural children and young people are heard;
- foster awareness of the rural dimension in Government policy development both at local and national levels;
- influence policy and practice with those planning services for children and young people in rural areas.

Families where there is a parent with mental ill health

Most projects offer support to children who are caring for parents with mental ill health. For some families it is the only support that they receive, particularly if they are anxious about contacting a statutory agency for help or do not meet the threshold criteria to receive services.

> "It is because mental illness is often regarded as a 'taboo' subject that many carers, especially young carers, may find themselves being stigmatised if it is known that a relative of theirs has a mental illness. The person for whom they care may be suicidal or violent or their moods can quickly change. This can be particularly stressful and frightening. The impact of caring for someone with mental illness can be emotionally exhausting."
> (Baker, PRTC, 2002)

> *"When she can't do stuff that she usually can do, or she stays in bed more than she usually would do, that's when I know she's really poorly or she starts moaning that she's seeing them, then I have to give her another tablet."*
> (Shah and Hatton, 1999)

Mental illness is often episodic. The situation at home can fluctuate from a normal secure home life to periods of instability, confusion and emotional upheaval. Changes in the behaviour of parents with mental ill health can be traumatic for the children, and all the more so if they are trying to take on some or all of the caring responsibilities. Children caring for a parent with mental ill health can feel a great sense of responsibility and loyalty to their parent and some go to great lengths to conceal the illness and its effects and to make up excuses for their behaviour.

MAKING IT WORK

Recognise that children may be undertaking care when the person who is ill does not meet eligibility criteria for a service, or when their condition is episodic. Have strategies in place to meet the needs of these children and their families.

"Children are even more conscious than adults of the stigma surrounding mental illness. For some their anxiety about potential stigmatising or bullying ensures that no one at school, either teachers or pupils, knows about their situation at home, and that no one ever visits them there."
(Wiltshire Young Carers' Strategy)

"I feel really guilty if I talk about her. I can't tell anyone because you can't trust people. So I keep it inside and it becomes a big secret. But then I snap and people don't know why. It's very difficult."
(Wiltshire Young Carers' Strategy)

Good practice

Good practice guidance for supporting families where a parent has mental ill health can be found in *Crossing Bridges: Training resources for working with mentally ill parents and their children* (Department of Health, 1998). Offering families timely and well-structured support could help prevent a child undertaking inappropriate care, particularly emotional care, and offer appropriate family-based support to any children who are already caring.

Key messages for agencies:

- **The needs of children and parents must be considered jointly.**
- **There is a need for a flexible range of services (long- and short-term) to support mentally ill parents and their children.**

Key messages for practitioners:

The parent's capacity to parent and children's welfare can be promoted by:

- **providing early treatment (effective access and outreach);**
- **promoting insight into illness and its implications;**
- **providing information about diagnosis, prognosis, services;**
- **promoting positive parenting including provision of practical support;**
- **working with the well parent and extended family;**

- ensuring intervention in Black families is culturally appropriate and is not an under- or over-reaction;
- helping the ill parent, other family members, and the child if appropriate, to plan for crises;
- providing practical support (housing, benefits, childcare) to reduce stress factors;
- reducing changes of careworkers and promoting continuity of care;
- developing parents' understanding of children's needs;
- identifying and meeting needs arising from separation and loss;
- helping parents to understand the illness (symptoms, treatment, ways of coping), its impact on their parenting and the impact on the child;
- agreeing with the parent what the child will be told about the illness;
- promoting open discussion about mental illness in the family where children can ask questions and parents can respond positively;
- encouraging and maintaining other positive and supportive relationships, including positive relationships and experiences at school.

Condensed from: *Crossing Bridges* (Department of Health, 1998)

MAKING IT WORK

Offering timely, well-structured and flexible support to the person in need of care could help prevent a child undertaking inappropriate levels of care.

Good practice examples

1. Gloucestershire Young Carers

Gloucestershire Young Carers set up a pilot therapeutic support group for young carers whose parents were suffering from chronic mental ill health, called the 'Us Too' Group.

The aims of the group were to:

- provide space where the group could identify and express feelings;
- reduce the sense of isolation by sharing experiences and views with others in a similar situation;
- enhance self-esteem and confidence;
- help children gain a greater understanding of their parents' illness and its impact on family life.

In addition to the therapeutic benefit, the group placed value on simply being listened to and taken seriously. A clear message from the children was that they should be consulted about and informed of decisions not only that affect their ill parent, but also that affect other family members. The need for schools to understand more about their needs was also clear, as it was at school that they felt the greatest need for secrecy.

continued overleaf

MAKING IT WORK

Foster communication:

- Inform children about family illness and changes to routine and circumstances at levels appropriate for child's age and understanding, regardless of whether they are caring or not.
- Work with the family to support them in talking about and coming to terms with illness, if needed.

2. Policy and practice recommendations

Aldridge and Becker (forthcoming publication, see below) of the Young Carers Research Group, Loughborough University, make recommendations about policy and practice for young carers whose parents have severe and enduring mental health problems, based on their research with 40 young carers, their parents and the professionals involved in these families.

Their findings suggest that statutory professionals in particular, and especially those working in adult mental health teams, rarely include children in discussions about their caring responsibilities, or consult with them about parents' treatment plans and family needs. Furthermore, formal needs assessments are rarely implemented for young carers in these contexts.

Aldridge and Becker propose mapping young carers' experiences and monitoring their needs using a formal device (which is fully explored in a dedicated chapter of the book) which would ensure that the children (young carers) of parents with severe mental health problems are not overlooked in terms of the services and support they need. (Aldridge, J. and Becker, S. (available 2003) *Children Caring for Parents with Mental Illness: The perspectives of young carers, parents and professionals.* Bristol: The Policy Press. A summary of the main findings is available from Centre for Child and Family Research (CCFR), Department of Social Sciences, Loughborough University, Leicestershire, LE11 3TU or from the CCFR website: www.ccfr.org.uk)

3. 'Keeping the Family in Mind'

In November 1999, a conference was held in Liverpool and Keeping the Family in Mind (I) was launched: a participative research project into mental ill health and how it affects the whole family. Four agencies worked together on the research: Mersey Care NHS Trust, IMAGIN (an adult mental health charity), Save the Children and Barnardo's Action with Young Carers, along with Liverpool University.

In June 2001, a development worker seconded from the Young Carers' Project and with 12 months' funding, began work on devising methods to implement the report's recommendations, ensuring they were participative and family-led.

The Project's aim is "to improve and enhance the range of appropriate, accessible, non-stigmatising and timely services to families with children, who are impacted by adult mental ill health in Liverpool". The Project set a number of objectives and tasks, and developments are now taking fruition. It is based in the Young Carers' Project and relies heavily on the experiences from work with young carers. Developments have included the establishment of a family room at a local psychiatric unit, where children and young people can visit their parents away from the ward in a relaxed, safe, welcoming environment. This involves joint working with children, young people, service users, the hospital trust, voluntary and statutory agencies.

Other developments include young carers designing a questionnaire to ensure their views are included under the National Service Framework Standard 6 on Carers, and designing a leaflet for Mersey Care NHS Trust. This followed the success of the Young Carers Mental Health Resource Pack, and a leaflet designed by children and young people whose parents have mental health problems. This provides information and graphics that the young people have produced and gives factual details about living with a parent who has mental health problems.

A clear strength has been the Multi-agency Advisory Group, whose key members have opened many doors and ensured the issues are taken seriously in their agencies.

MAKING IT WORK

Promote more open discussion and provide accessible 'family-friendly' literature about mental ill health and how to access help.

Resources for work with families where a parent has mental ill health

- **Rethink** (formerly National Schizophrenia Fellowship) has a website for young people which is for, by and about young people.

Rethink website:
www.at-ease.nsf.org.uk

- **Young Minds** provides information to young people about mental ill health.Their publication *Mental illness in the family?* explains what mental illness is, the different kinds of mental illness and symptoms. It also looks at the causes of mental illness, and the impact that it has on other family members. The booklet includes details of a number of helping organisations and is free from Young Minds.

  Parents' Information Service 0800 018 2138 (Mon. & Fri 10am – 1pm, Tue – Thu 1pm – 4pm)

  email: info@youngminds.org.uk

Young Minds website:
www.youngminds.org.uk

- *Crossing Bridges: Training Resources for working with mentally ill parents and their children.* Department of Health, 1998.

Refugees

(See also Chapter 3, page 44 for a discussion of how the specific needs of refugees and asylum-seekers can be addressed.).

> "Refugee communities share a number of problems. These include language difficulties and 'culture-shock', feelings of isolation, vulnerability and stress. Refugees have all faced persecution in one form or another, and suffer varying degrees of physical and psychological trauma; some may also have been tortured. In addition, refugees often feel insecure because of separation from their families and their uncertain legal status. Inevitably, mental health is the single most important health problem affecting refugees. It is important that medical staff should be aware of the patient's refugee background before diagnosis and treatment. Likewise, it is important for staff to be trained in refugee health."
>
> Source: Karmi, G. (1996) *The Ethnic Health Handbook: A fact-file for Health Care Professionals.* Blackwell Science

A Case for Change: First findings of the monitoring project of the refugees' children's consortium (May 2002) points out that:

> "Refugees and asylum seekers have full equal entitlements to health service regardless of status."

It also states that:

> "Primary and health care trusts should ensure that GPs providing a service to refugees are able to provide equal access, and in particular should use an interpreter when necessary."

In areas where registrations are particularly problematic, flexible options should be employed to improve the situation.

In the Refugee Council's Response to the Government's White Paper *Secure Borders, Safe Haven*, it welcomes the proposal to offer health assessments to all newly arrived asylum-seekers and points out that this would have the clear benefits of identifying any special needs and access to health care if needed. It advocates that procedures would need to be developed to ensure that people with disabilities are swiftly allocated specialist care.

MAKING IT WORK

The needs of refugee families who have a family member who is disabled or has mental health needs should be considered when allocation of housing or dispersal is being considered.

Issues for refugee carers overlap with those of young carers generally. In supporting refugee children who may be caring for a relative, it is important to remember that young people caring for a relative because of disability or ill health will not necessarily have the support of their community. This is particularly so if the family has been dispersed to an area of the country with no established community group. They could be less likely to be linked in with support groups, and may in fact feel very differently about support from formal sources because of cultural expectations of their role or of a different perception of the duty to look after their elders.

There are also many young people who, having arrived in the UK as two siblings, are not supported as unaccompanied children and therefore cared for by the local authority social services, but instead are treated as a family group. This means that an elder sibling acts as the parent of a younger sibling. (Source: Refugee Council)

Resources for working with refugees

The Department of Health has issued an information and resource pack on refugees and asylum-seekers which includes a section on eligibility for and provision of health services.

Website:
www.london.nhs.uk/newsmedia/publications.htm

Drug misuse and alcohol dependency

Many young carers' projects support children caring for someone who misuses drugs or is dependent on alcohol. They often work with local specialist agencies to provide support to both child and family. Remember that many of these families and children will feel anxious about revealing their problems and taking the first steps to seeking help. Children will often recognise the need for help before their parents. It is important that children and young people are aware of who they can turn to for help and have plans in place for crisis intervention.

MAKING IT WORK

Children may be aware that help is needed for their parent or for themselves before the parent has recognised the need. Agencies need to ensure that information about how to seek advice and support is accessible to children.

Drug use

(Details of assessments for young carers of drug-using parents can be found in Chapter 3.)

Research by Tunnard (2002) highlights the importance of giving children:

- opportunities both to understand and escape from the stresses they experience;
- reassurance that they are not to blame for their parents' problems and that it is not their responsibility to resolve adult conflict or take on a caring role beyond their years;
- help to cope with any losses they may suffer when they have to stay away from home, or their parents are in treatment or prison;
- reassurance that they will not be removed from their family;
- opportunities for group discussion and activities;
- play and leisure opportunities, which can enable them to enjoy themselves, improve social skills with their peers and gain confidence to discuss worries with trusted adults;
- help to cope with any changes at home as result of parents benefiting from drug and parenting programmes.

MAKING IT WORK

Provide support to meet identified parenting needs.

A report published by the Liverpool Health Authority (Liverpool Health and Alcohol Team, 2001) highlighted some implications for practice:

- Adult services need to become family-centred to accommodate the fact that a substantial number of their service users are parents.
- Services should be child-friendly. This means resources and facilities as well as a kind attitude, which is greatly appreciated by children.
- Integration and coordination of adult and child services must be improved. Children's workers should work within adult service teams and vice versa. Multi-agency working is essential.
- Services should make efforts to contribute to a reduction in stigma and establish more open and trusting relationships with service users. Parents need to be confident that they will receive non-judgemental support. Parents and children also need to be able to understand social services interventions and guidelines for confidentiality.
- More involvement from service users and their children is required to help direct service change and improvement.
- Affected children are profoundly isolated, and services that can be directly accessed by children need to be increased.

MAKING IT WORK

Ensure family and children know how to access help in a crisis.

Good practice examples

STARS

STARS, a project established by The Children's Society, is developing a support project for families in Nottingham. It aims:

- to prevent the cycle of substance use within families by:
  - addressing the impact of substance use upon the child;
  - supporting the child in the development of their own coping mechanisms;
  - enabling children and young people to have an insight into the impacts of substance use;
  - exploring systemic family issues with the child.
- to prevent, where possible, the removal of children from their families and community by:
  - ensuring early assessment and services are offered;
  - offering a consultancy service for social workers undertaking assessments where a referral has not been accepted due to the length of the waiting list.

Andover Young Carers

Andover Young Carers, in Hampshire, has received funding for a full-time support worker to support children with parents who have drug, alcohol or mental health problems. The post has been created because of the large numbers of referrals the Project received

from the local Drug and Alcohol Agency, together with a low rate of referrals from the Community Mental Health Team. Although all the referrals from the Drug and Alcohol Agency have been included in the mainstream group activities of the Project, the behavioural and emotional needs of these children have been far more demanding than the majority of the other young carers. The new support worker's role is to enable one-to-one contact time with these children and their families.

This one-to-one time is initially being used to enable the young carer to pursue a new hobby that requires focus, listening and practice. The Project is currently funding golf, music and horse-riding lessons, which are also supported by 'Buddies' (adult befrienders). The initial series of lessons will be followed by group sessions to support the young carers' behavioural development. The Project also spends time with the parents to encourage them to look at their parenting skills and the effect that their drug use is having on their children. Although in its early stages, this new Project is already showing signs of success. The increase in the children's self-esteem is noticeable as they experience the thrill of mastering new skills and making measurable progress.

Resources

Organisations that can offer support to children whose parent has alcohol or drug dependency include National Association for Children of Alcoholics, Alateen and ADFAM.

See also

Cleaver H., Unell, I. and Aldgate J. (1999) *Children's Needs – Parenting Capacity: The impact of parental mental illness, problem alcohol and drug use, and domestic violence on children's development.* London: The Stationery Office.

An exploration of the research literature shows that these potential problems affect children differently depending on their age and individual circumstances.

Harbin, F. and Murphy, M. (eds) (2000) *Substance Misuse and Childcare: How to understand, assist and intervene when drugs affect parenting.* Russell House Publishing.

Hogg, C., Chadwick, T. and Dale-Perera, A. (1997) *Drug-using Parents: Policy guidelines for inter-agency working.* London: Local Government Association.

HIV/AIDS

Children whose parents have AIDS or are living with HIV will need sensitive and specialist support. Families will need support so that the child does not undertake inappropriate levels of care.

The particular nature of the illness, associated stigma and need for confidentiality may compound to hide the level of caring that a child is undertaking, particularly at an emotional level. Projects do support these children when referred, but they work in partnership with specialist health personnel and social services teams.

Resources

- The Terrence Higgins Trust is the national HIV organisation that can offer advice and information.
- The helpline: 020 7242 1010 can offer practical support, help, counselling and advice for anyone with or concerned about AIDS and HIV infection.
- There are also many local organisations that also offer support to these families and children.

Loss and bereavement

There are a number of specialist national organisations that can offer children support during bereavement. It is important not to rely solely on these specialist agencies but to consider how your agency or group or school can support a child with whom you already have contact during bereavement.

Helping a child cope with the process of bereavement:

- **Do acknowledge the loss.**
- **Reach out to the child.**
- **Take and make time to listen.**
- **Avoid any comments that may sound insincere and avoid relating to your own experiences.**
- **Do not pressurise.**
- **Remember the child may feel alone and isolated.**
- **Remember that bereavement is a process that takes place over time and that can affect individuals in different ways and over differing timescales.**

Source: Holland, J. *Coping with Bereavement: A handbook for teachers.* Cardiff: Academic Press.

MAKING IT WORK

Ensure that children can still access their projects or support groups following bereavement.

Resources

- Cruse Bereavement Care Helpline: 0870 167 1677
- Sources of help and information on any specific illness or condition can be obtained from NHS Direct.
- Other sources of help are listed in the Bibliography.

Cruse Bereavement Care website: **www.crusebereavementcare.org.uk**

CHAPTER 7
The Role of Young Carers' Projects

Introduction

This chapter looks at the role that young carers' projects have in supporting children and families, and includes some guidelines that will be useful for those setting up new services or developing new resources in existing services, either in projects or in mainstream or other voluntary sector provision.

> *"...It's knowing that there is all this group behind you – there when you are feeling a bit low and all you have to do is phone someone up and you know that you have always got people stood behind you, who are caring for you...."*
>
> (Young carer)

Projects that have evolved across the UK to meet local needs offer a range of direct services to young carers and their families. Many projects have been offering support for a number of years and have a wealth of expertise about young carers' issues and local needs. Evaluations show that the services provided are greatly valued by both the children and their families. Peer support offered by young carers' groups is greatly valued by the children. Many young carers say how isolated they feel and that meeting others in the same situation really helps.

MAKING IT WORK

Young carers say they value the peer support they receive when attending projects.

> *"Before I felt alone, now at meetings I've got people to talk to. I've made new friends."*

Projects also play a key role in raising awareness, offering training and identifying gaps in services, not just for young carers but also for the person in need of care and for other agencies who offer services.

> *"They [projects] give the carer an outlet, a bolt hole. It gives them someone else they can turn to and it also brings out the fact that there is a need to support young carers to show how valuable they really are and that they are not taken for granted... It also gives the young carer an interest outside the home, somewhere to go where somebody sympathises and understands what their problems are."*
>
> (Parent)

Setting up a new project or developing new resources

When setting up new projects or resources for young carers and their families, it is advisable to draw on the experience and knowledge of other agencies in the field and to involve potential users in the planning stages. The following is a guide to the steps that need to be taken:

- **Identify the needs of the potential user group.**
- **Identify existing services accessible to young carers and their families and decide whether these can be developed further.**
- **Set the aims, objectives and projected outcomes of the intended service to meet the needs of users.**
- **Make sure that your plans conform to current legislation and guidance.**
- **Plan the organisational structure:**
  - **Independent/voluntary or statutory sector**
  - **Funding streams**
  - **Management structures**
  - **Steering group membership**
  - **Working policies (see 'policy documents' below)**
  - **Strategies for inter-agency and holistic practice**
  - **Partnerships with other services – identify any known links or any that need to be developed**
- **Practice issues:**
  - **Staffing requirements – experience and qualifications**
  - **Training needs**
  - **Resource needs, including venues and transport**
  - **Reaching the identified user group: awareness-raising, information, communication channels, accountability, monitoring and evaluation.**

Existing projects in the local area (or a similar area) may be able to assist with gathering information by undertaking local research, consultation and an audit of needs, which can be used to inform the shape of the new or increased service.

Policy documents

As with all childcare work, a set of policies will be needed to underpin and guide the work. Suggested policies are listed below. It would be good practice to review and update these policies on a regular basis.

MAKING IT WORK

Consider how funding partnerships can support work with young carers and their families (e.g. Early Years Children's Fund, Sure Start, Connexions).

MAKING IT WORK

Involve young people and families in planning services at all stages of development.

Suggested policy documents for young carers' support services and projects

Policies related to services offered:

- Advocacy
- Befriending or mentoring
- Group activities
- Project accident and incident sheets
- Media work

Policies related to project users:

- Child protection
- Charging policy
- Confidentiality policy and statement
- Consent forms
- Eligibility criteria
- Risk assessment
- Complaints procedures for users
- Quality assurance and evaluation

Policies relating to staffing:

- Volunteer policy
- Equal opportunities and anti-discrimination
- Health and safety guidelines
- Guidelines for management committee members
- General guidelines for staff and volunteers
- Guidance rules for staff, befrienders and volunteers (who take children and young people out)
- Staff recruitment and appointments
- Complaints procedure for staff and volunteers
- Discipline/ grievance procedure for staff and volunteers
- Record keeping
- Transport policy
- Training requirements
- Internet use

MAKING IT WORK

Ensure all workers understand and adhere to the organisation's guidelines about disclosure of information and that young people understand the confidentiality policy.

Criminal Records Bureau

The Criminal Records Bureau (CRB) has been set up by the Home Office to improve access to criminal records checks for employment-related purposes. The CRB will undertake criminal records checks for individuals, on application, in exchange for a fee. It will issue three types of certificate, each representing a different level of check. The level of check will be determined by the duties of the job or position to be taken up.

Those working or volunteering for work with young carers will qualify for the most detailed check. This check will contain details of all convictions on record, including those 'spent' under the Rehabilitation of Offenders Act 1974. This means that even minor convictions will be included on the certificate. It will also contain details of any cautions, reprimands and warnings recorded against a person.

Where a job or voluntary role involves close contact with children, the check will also contain details of whether the applicant is named on the lists held by the Department for Education and Skills and the Department of Health of those unsuitable to work with children. In addition, the certificate may contain information held by the police that is not about convictions, but which they feel is relevant to the job or voluntary post. It is possible to access the CRB process through an umbrella body. More information can be found at www.crb.gov.uk

Criminal Records Bureau website:
www.crb.gov.uk

Training and qualifications

Agencies need to ensure that staff have appropriate qualifications and skills to support children and families and to engage in direct work. It is important that they offer appropriate training to enable staff to support young carers and their families effectively. Training will need to be offered according to the aims of the project or service and the needs of users and staff. However, basic training should include:

- Child protection
- Disabilty issues
- Equal opportunities and anti-discrimination
- Group work
- Listening skills
- Legislation
- Risk assessment

Awareness-raising

There are two key elements to awareness-raising. One is to promote awareness of need, responsibilities and available support and services to all relevant agencies in contact with young carers or with families where there may be young carers.

The second is to promote awareness among families and children of how to access assessments and services.

Raising awareness among agencies

This can be done through:

- written materials, leaflets, posters and newsletters;
- agency team meetings, awaydays and training events;
- users assisting with planning of local policy and practice provision;
- resource packs for schools
- videos (see Bibliography)
- websites (see pp. 54–55)

MAKING IT WORK

Awareness-raising of the needs of young carers and their families needs a multi-agency approach and should include both adults' and children's services.

Good practice example

Norfolk County Council Social Services has produced a review of services available for young carers in the format of a full-colour newsletter using the words of young carers. This is also used to inform agencies.

Raising awareness of services available for users

Encourage users (both young carers and their families) to access services by raising awareness of what these can offer:

- provide well-targeted, accessible information (presentation, content and language need to be child- and family-friendly);
- offer safe environments so they feel able to approach an agency for help;
- promote more positive images of disability and illness;
- acknowledge and support parenting needs;
- encourage user involvement in planning processes and informing content of information leaflets;
- ensure children have opportunities to talk to someone;
- listen to children, believe and understand;
- avoid being judgmental;
- ensure services are culturally sensitive;
- work to an agreed confidentiality policy.

MAKING IT WORK

Agencies need to consider how they will review, monitor and evaluate the services they provide. The Quality Protects initiative provides a framework for services to evaluate and monitor performance.

Further resources

Factor, Chauhan and Pitts, PRTC (2001) give detailed guidance on setting up a young carers' project and practical advice on the day-to-day running of a service. Although written primarily for use in Scotland, it is a valuable tool for anyone setting up or running a service.

Other resources which have helpful guidance for setting up young carers' projects include:

Russell House Publishing (2001) *The RHP Companion to Working with Young People.*

Ingram, G. and Harris, J. (2001) *Delivering Good Youth Work: A working guide to surviving and thriving.* Russell House Publishing

The Internet is an excellent source of information and a number of websites have been developed to support young carers and advise those who work to support them. See pages 54–55 for examples.

Support for families and the person in need of care

> *"Just knowing they [the young carers' project] care and understand. It helps us and so we can all pull together as one big family."*
>
> (Parent and care receiver)

Most young carers' projects endeavour, subject to resource constraints, to support families in a number of ways. The following list illustrates some services that are offered by projects:

- Promoting awareness of the needs of families where someone has a disability or illness.
- Advocacy on behalf of the person who needs care, to access information and services.
- Regular social opportunities for both children and families.
- Enabling lone parents to go to leisure facilities with their child accompanied by a befriender. (The befriender does not offer care but may provide transport and support with parenting – for example, in ensuring the child's safety.)

> *"They [project] have helped get a worker to do the work at home. This has helped me in getting on with my school work and improved my mum's health."*
>
> *"I hope the project doesn't have to stop...It helps us all."*
>
> (Parent and care receiver)

MAKING IT WORK

Work with the family and seek to advocate for services to support the person in need of care as well as supporting the young carer.

Arranging respite care

Some projects work in partnership with other organisations (e.g. Crossroads for Carers) to arrange extra care in the home while the child attends a young carers' group or residential activity. This is usually organised by the care worker responsible for the person needing care. The British Red Cross has been piloting a scheme to provide domiciliary care in the home/sitting service so that the children can go out to groups and activities of their choice.

Group work

Group work provides a valuable resource for young carers, enabling them to meet together and explore common issues, and offering both professional and peer support. It also provides the young carer with opportunities to have time away from any pressures, stress and responsibilities.

The majority of young carers' projects offer group work in various ways:

- drop-in resources
- after-school and homework clubs
- training workshops such as first aid and risk assessment
- stress-busting, healthcare and therapy sessions
- dealing with bullying
- confidence-building, self-advocacy
- leisure activities
- gaining new skills
- drama and theatre group work
- arts work
- IT skills
- siblings groups

MAKING IT WORK

Venues and activities need to conform to Local Authority guidelines and standards. Groups providing support to children aged under eight will be subject to regulations and inspections by OFSTED.

Young carers say the group activities give them the chance to:

- meet others in the same situation and gain peer support;
- feel less isolated;
- have someone to talk to;
- access emotional support;
- learn new skills and leisure opportunities;
- build confidence;
- access information;
- feel recognised and valued;
- have a voice and be consulted about their needs and those of their families.

> *"It hasn't taken away from me as a parent. In fact I feel like I'm gaining and the children are gaining...When the kids come home after an evening out with the group, they are happy and full of beans, they are bouncy. It just raises their spirits."*
> (Mother and care receiver)

Befriending and mentoring schemes

> *"Being a befriender is very useful, not only to the young carers but also to all the family. You are in a very privileged position as the child and parents rely on you for support and sharing of information."*
>
> (Befriender, Winchester)

A number of young carers' projects have established a befriending or mentoring scheme. These provide opportunities for young carers to talk and be listened to on a one-to-one basis. Befriending can be of particular support for young carers who are facing imminent bereavement, those who are experiencing emotional anxiety, stress or depression, those who lack the confidence or do not wish to join a group for support, and those who feel particularly isolated. Evaluation of befriending schemes shows that young carers' self-confidence and social skills increase.

MAKING IT WORK

Services offering emotional support need to be sensitive to individual needs of the child and the family and offer continuity and an exit strategy.

Key principles for setting up a volunteer befriending scheme

- Make contact with other projects that have a befriending/mentoring scheme and learn from their experience.
- Set clear aims and objectives, which are achievable and manageable.
- Identify resources and set your budget.
- Have clear, written policy documents for the scheme.
- Design clear information for the volunteers to include a post description, basic information about your organisation, a list of tasks to be undertaken, time needed, information about expenses, tralning, supervision and support.
- Design a person specification, including the knowledge, skills, qualities, experience and motivation that you require from the volunteer.
- It is essential to interview volunteers and voluntary work should only be offered subject to suitable references, police checks and successful completion of training.
- Undertake a criminal records check (see p. 108).
- Ensure that you have adequate insurance cover to protect volunteers and your organisation.
- It is important that training is provided for volunteers to develop the skills, understanding and insight they need in their role as a befriender.
- Training needs to be well planned, informative and enjoyable.
- It is essential to evaluate the effectiveness of the training and to adapt it as necessary.

Practice procedures

Initial visit

- On receiving a referral, try to ensure the initial visit is made with the practitioner who referred the family. If the person referred is not in regular contact with the family, or is the young carer, the initial contact should be made by the befriending coordinator alone. This contact should be made by telephone and confirmed in writing, setting out the time, date and purpose of the visit.

Contact agreement form

- Ensure the contact agreement form is clearly filled out and signed by the volunteer and parent of the young carer. Ensure that all parties understand and agree with the information contained in the form.
- From the outset, it must be made clear that withdrawal is an option at any time in the befriending relationship, although the befriender must give due notice. It is important that reasons for withdrawal are discussed with the co-ordinator.

Monitoring, evaluation and review

- Regular monitoring and reviewing by the coordinator is essential to ensure the good practice and success of the befriending scheme. For example, the Winchester Young Carers' Project carries out an initial review after one month, then at three-monthly intervals, with regular telephone contact with all involved. A written report is kept of all these meetings.
- The process of evaluation should be built into all stages of the work, as it enables the project to be accountable to the young carers and families worked with. Reviewing, monitoring and evaluation enable the project to identify strengths and weaknesses and so improve practice.

Recording visits

- Diary sheets giving brief details about the visit should be filled in by the volunteer and young carer, and signed by the parent.

Supervision

- If the befriender is dealing with complex issues, individual supervision should be given.
- Group supervision should form part of any befriending/mentoring scheme, as this enables the coordinator and volunteers to keep in touch with the befriending relationship and the project as a whole.

Source: Taylor (1999)

Resources to assist with setting up a befriending scheme

- Taylor, A. (1999) *Developing a Befriending Scheme: A toolkit for practitioners.* London: The Children's Society (see Bibliography for further details).
- Willow Young Carers Befriending Scheme – particular experience of supporting young carers of someone with mental health problems
- YCRG (1994) *A Friend in Need: The case for befriending young carers*
- The Terrence Higgins Trust

Links with Youth Work

Youth work with young carers can provide valuable support for their own personal, social and educational development. Many projects work in partnership with local Youth Service initiatives and some are located within the statutory Youth Service provision.

MAKING IT WORK

Other resources (e.g. drama, art therapy, workshops) can give young people a chance to express their thoughts and feelings and get messages across.

UK Youth

The aim of the UK Youth Programme is to initiate and develop nationwide projects that address many of the special needs of young people who have taken on the responsibility of looking after members of their family who may require additional support.

The Programme itself aims to raise awareness of the existence and needs of young carers within the statutory and voluntary youth work sectors and also to enthuse and empower youth workers to establish young carers' social clubs and support groups within community settings. The project is managed by the National UK Youth Work Director and involves local associations and associate member organisations throughout the country.

UK Youth has also produced a training guide based on the perspectives of young carers (UK Youth, 2001), which contains photocopiable activities to raise awareness of the surrounding issues. Guidelines on facilitating these activities are also included. (See Bibliography.)

Good practice examples:

Initiatives and links with the Youth Service have been developed by many projects.

York and Selby Young Carers

York and Selby Young Carers have received Youth Awards and attend York Youth Forum. Joint work is planned within one of the local schools.

Harrogate and Craven

Harrogate and Cravens runs several evening and lunchtime clubs in partnership with Community Education (the local name for the service that encompasses the Youth Service). Community Education provide workers, transport and venues; the Project provides in-depth young carer training for their workers, finds funding for resources that is often not open to statutory sector agencies, and provides activities during school holidays when the clubs are closed.

Bolton

Bolton has strong links with the Youth Service, who provide a programme of activities over the summer and in school holidays for young carers accessing the Project.

Norfolk

Crossroads Norfolk Young Carers' Project works in partnership with the Youth Service to deliver several young carers' groups across the county. The Project says that partnership with the Youth Service means excellent trained personnel, premises, minibus and access to other services run by them.

Bournemouth

Bournemouth has Youth Workers co-working with a Girls' Group, and the Lads' Group is currently run by the Youth Service.

Advocacy

Advocacy is a valuable service for supporting families and young people. If a parent is debilitated, vulnerable or finds communication difficult because of their illness, an advocacy service may be able to assist them in accessing information, support and services. Young carers can also benefit from an advocacy service that helps them articulate their own needs and understand systems and jargon. Advocacy can support people in speaking for themselves or in presenting their views for them, and assist them in making informed and free choices.

Many young carers' projects offer advocacy to both families and the young carers. Some projects provide the service themselves, while others work in partnership with local youth service advocacy schemes and independent advocacy services, assisting with communication with statutory agencies including housing, benefits and schools.

Advocacy services can provide practical assistance and support for young carers and their families by:

- assessing whether families are receiving all the services that should be available for them;

- contributing to assessments and care planning;
- mediation work;
- helping them to complete forms (benefits, housing, etc);
- writing letters, speaking on their behalf, attending meetings, etc;
- facilitating/improving lines of communication between agencies and service providers to improve inter-agency working.

In a wider context, advocacy by the project and its members can help the development of services.

MAKING IT WORK

Providing advocacy is a skill and staff will need to be trained in order to be effective advocates.

Counselling

Some young carers will benefit from counselling. This may be provided by a project, if qualified staff members are available or can be accessed from a local statutory or voluntary service. Child and Mental Health Services should be able to offer access to counselling for young carers who are assessed as needing this service. Any cultural needs should also be taken into account.

MAKING IT WORK

Any service offering counselling should be provided only by accredited, qualified professionals.

The value of projects

For many children and their families, young carers' projects have been their only or main source of support, particularly in terms of providing information, advocacy and someone who will listen to the child and support their developmental needs if required. Support from projects has been valued by both young people and their families.

Project staff have empowered young carers to feel able to seek support for themselves and, in turn, have highlighted the need for more flexible and effective support in the home which would prevent them from undertaking inappropriate levels of care.

Over the past decade, the young people, their families and project staff have helped to shape many local policies through a range of consultation processes. Obtaining funding in order to continue to provide services to meet identified needs and demands takes up a large amount of project staff time. Some projects constantly face closure and work under very difficult circumstances.

It is important that both funders and policy-makers:

- recognise the collective expertise that has been established in so many different projects across the UK;
- review the impact that these projects have had on supporting young carers and their families;
- consider how best to move forwards in order to meet the needs of young carers and their families in a holistic and equitable approach.

MAKING IT WORK

It is important to recognise the existing skill base in establish-ed projects and to look at how holistic and comprehensive services can be further developed using this experience and knowledge.

Future Development

Those of us who are directly involved in work with young carers are fully aware that such work represents something of a journey.

Even ten years ago, the issues facing young carers were largely unrecognised. In the interim, responses to these issues have evolved in line with the development of a more sophisticated analysis of young carers' needs. More recently has come recognition of the need to understand young carers' needs within the context of the whole family, together with the need to ensure that agency and project responses to meeting these needs are planned and delivered coherently.

There exists today a growing recognition by government departments of the needs of young carers and their families, and a movement towards ensuring that policy and practice guidelines recognise those areas where statutory agencies have a role to play in meeting such needs.

It is clear that levels of understanding, together with direct practice experience, will continue to evolve and develop in the future. This Practice Guide represents what is understood about best practice at this point in time. It owes its existence to the contributions made by young carers, their families, and the professionals involved in working with them.

What is important for the future is that we continue this journey together. It is only through continuing dialogue and the modelling and sharing of what works best for young carers and their families, that their needs will be met more completely and appropriately.

Appendix

Annotated Bibliography

Annotated Bibliography

This bibliography contains publications used as references throughout the practice guide and other publications and resources that may be useful. It is organised under subject headings containing: books/reports for professionals; other resources for professionals; and books/ resources for use with young people.

Young Carers

Books for professionals

Aldridge, J. and Becker, S. (1993)
Children Who Care: Inside the world of young carers.
Loughborough University: Young Carers Research Group.

An original piece of research undertaken in Nottingham, which gives a detailed account of the lives and experiences of child carers, often using their own words. Biographies of the children and detailed descriptions of their caring duties are included, along with: a discussion of the effects of caring; suggestions of ways forward for professionals and policy makers; and a list of young carers' rights.

Aldridge, J. and Becker, S. (1994a)
My Child, My Carer: The parents' perspective.
Loughborough University: Young Carers Research Group.

This is a follow-up report to *Children who Care* and discusses the issue of caring from the point of view of the adults who are cared for by their children. It is intended as a companion volume to the first report.

Aldridge, J. and Becker, S. (1994b)
A Friend Indeed: The case for befriending young carers.
Loughborough University: Young Carers Research Group.

Many young carers have said that they would like someone to talk to. This report describes the principles and guidelines necessary for the safe implementation of a befriending service for young carers. It includes discussion of recruitment practices, child protection issues and the training of volunteers.

Aldridge, J. and Becker, S. (1995b)
'The Rights and Wrongs of Children Who Care', in Franklin, B. (ed.) *The Handbook of Children's Rights: Comparative policy and practice.*
London: Routledge.

A discussion of the way in which young carers have been 'constructed' by the media and others, and how they may be 'reconstructed' in a manner suited to ensuring their rights as children and as carers are met.

Aldridge, J. and Becker, S. (1996a)
Befriending Young Carers: A pilot study.
Loughborough University: Young Carers Research Group.

Describes the practical application of the strategies outlined in *A Friend Indeed* and reports the results of a pilot project, which linked volunteer befrienders and young carers. Useful for those planning befriending services for children.

Aldridge, J. and Becker, S. (1996b)
'Disability rights and the denial of young carers – the dangers of zero-sum arguments', in *Critical Social Policy,* 16 (3) issue 48, 1996, pp. 55–76.

Aldridge, J. and Becker, S. (1997)
Prevention and Intervention: Young carers and their families.
Loughborough University: Young Carers Research Group.

A theoretical analysis of the strategies for preventing young caring in the community, and a discussion of programmes for intervention when young caring is already established within families.

Aldridge, J. and Becker, S. (1998)
The National Handbook of Young Carers' Projects.
London: Carers National Association.

Updated from the 1995 *Directory of Young Carers' Projects and Initiatives*. The Handbook includes information on 110 young carers' projects across the UK as well as profiles of the work practices of a selection of these projects.

Aldridge, J. and Becker, S. (1999)
'Children as carers: the impact of parental illness and disability on children's caring roles' in *Journal of Family Therapy*, Vol. 21 pp. 303–320.

Alexander, H. (1995)
Young Carers and HIV.
Edinburgh: Children in Scotland.

A small-scale research study looking at children who are affected by HIV/AIDS in the family. This is the first piece of work to look specifically at young carers and HIV.

Baker, G. (2002)
Unseen and Unheard: The invisible young carers.
Carers Lewisham, Princess Royal Trust for Carers.

Based on the work of the Carers Lewisham Young Carers' Schools Development project.

Banks, P. et al. (2002)
Young Carers: Assessment and service literature review of identification, needs assessment and service provision for young carers and their families.
Scottish Executive Central Research Unit

Available from the Scottish Executive website at: www.scotland.gov.uk

Becker, S. (ed.) (1995)
Young Carers in Europe: An exploratory cross-national study in Britain, France, Sweden and Germany.
Loughborough University: Young Carers Research Group in association with the European Research Centre.

A study of the experiences of young carers in four European countries, with a discussion about the attitudes of professionals working with children and families; and a discussion of the welfare regimes in the four countries. This exploratory study suggests that Britain's welfare system is more developed in its response to young caring both in policy and practice.

Becker, S., Aldridge, J. and Dearden, C. (1998)
Young Carers and their Families.
Oxford: Blackwell Science.

A comprehensive text on young carers and their families that is both research-based and adopts an international perspective. The book discusses the effects of caring on children's health and development and considers the policy and legal context, offering guidance on how to implement the most appropriate support.

Bibby, A. and Becker, S. (eds.) (2000)
Young Carers in their Own Words.
London: Calouste Gulbenkian Foundation.

The first part of this text presents written accounts by children and young people of what it is like to care. Most of them were in contact with locally-based young carers' projects. The second part considers issues of public policy. Also provides good practice checklists.

Bilsborrow, S. (1992)
"You grow up fast as well..." Young Carers on Merseyside.
Liverpool: Carers National Association, Personal Services Society and Barnardo's.

This was the first research study to examine the experiences and needs of young carers. The report includes quotes from young carers and a discussion from the perspective of welfare professionals.

Blyth, E. and Milner, J. (1997)
Social Work with Children: The educational perspective.
Harlow: Longman.

As the title suggests, this book takes an educational perspective on social work, but contains a chapter entitled 'Children who care for others', which gives an overview of some of the literature and research into young carers' issues.

Blyth, E. and Waddell, A. (1999)
'Young carers – the contradictions of being a child carer', in *Children, Child Abuse and Child Protection. Placing Children Centrally*, Chapter 2.
Chichester: John Wiley and Sons Ltd

Brechin, A. et al. (eds) (1998)
Care Matters: Concepts, practice and research in health and social care.
London: Sage.

A comprehensive text on care, useful for anyone working in social care or with informal carers. Contains a chapter on young carers by Stan Tucker and Penny Liddiard of the Open University, based on their research in Milton Keynes and Wolverhampton.

The Children's Society (2000)
Young Carers and Our Families – Report.

A transcript of a presentation by young carers, written by the young carers themselves, to Community Care Live 2000 about their lives and messages to practitioners.

(Video also available – see resources section below)

Clarke, E. (1996)
Young Carers in Guildford – Seeing the Whole.
Guildford Crossroads and Surrey Social Services.

Crabtree, H. and Warner, L. (1999)
Too Much to Take On: A report on young carers and bullying.
London: The Princess Royal Trust for Carers.

Looks at the problems young carers face at school with regard to bullying. Young carers are frequently isolated from their peers due to the amount of time they spend at home with the person they care for. This increases their vulnerability to bullying. This report finds that most young carers are likely to experience some form of bullying during their school career and may find it difficult to seek help and support. The report concludes with a series of recommendations.

Dearden, C. and Becker, S. (1995)
Young Carers: The Facts.
Reed Business Publishing.

The first ever national survey of young carers, this research includes information on more than 600 young carers who are supported by designated young carers' projects across the UK. Included is information relating to the age, gender, ethnicity, family structure and caring responsibilities of young carers, and details about the people they are caring for. In addition to statistical information, the research also includes material from interviews with young carers and project workers.

Dearden, C. and Becker, S. (1996)
Young Carers at the Crossroads: An evaluation of the Nottingham Young Carers' Project.
Loughborough University: Young Carers Research Group.

An evaluation of the Nottingham project that includes information about the project's location, management and staffing and the services it provides. The report also contains a profile of the Nottingham young carers and those for whom they care. The project is evaluated against its own aims and objectives; against guidelines for projects; and through interviews with young carers, their parents and professionals who have referred children to the project.

Dearden, C. and Becker, S. (1997)
Children in Care, Children who Care: Parental illness and disability and the child care system.
Loughborough University: Young Carers Research Group.

This report examines the incidence of children looked after because of parental illness and suggests ways of supporting families in order to prevent children's admission to the public child care system.

Dearden, C. and Becker, S. (1998)
Young Carers in the United Kingdom: A profile.
London: Carers National Association.

A survey of 2,303 young carers supported by designated projects around the UK. The research offers a statistical profile of young carers including information about age, gender, ethnicity, caring roles and responsibilities. In addition the research examines the assessment of young carers under the Carers and Children Acts. Contains statistical information and case studies.

Dearden, C., and Becker, S. (2000a)
Growing Up Caring: Vulnerability and transition to adulthood – young carers' experiences.
York: Joseph Rowntree Foundation.

Findings of a study of 60 young people with responsibility for caring for a parent with an illness or disability, and their experience of transition to adulthood. Identifies factors associated with caring that affect transition.

Dearden, C. and Becker, S. (2000b)
'Young Carers: Needs, Rights and Assessments' in Horwath, J. (Ed) *The Child's World: Assessing Children's Needs. The Reader.*
London: Department of Health.

This reader accompanies the Department of Health's new framework for assessing children. The chapter looks specifically at assessing young carers.

Department of Health (Feb 2000)
Quality Standards for Local Carer Support Services.

Factor, F., Chauhan, V. and Pitts, J. (2001)
Young Carers Good Practice Guide.
London: Princess Royal Trust for Carers.

A good practice guide for setting up a young carers' project based on the experiences of a number of projects in Scotland.

Frank, J. (1995)
Couldn't Care More: A study of young carers and their needs.
London: The Children's Society.

A study of 91 young carers in Winchester, a semi-rural area. The study identifies young carers' needs, discusses the outcomes of caring and makes recommendations for future practice. The words of young carers are used throughout the report. The research led to the implementation of the Winchester Young Carers' Project.

Frank, J., Tatum, C. and Tucker, S. (1999)
On Small Shoulders: Learning from the experiences of former young carers.
London: The Children's Society.

Hampshire County Council Social Services Department (2000)
Taking Responsibility: Inter-agency policy for supporting young carers.
Hampshire County Council.

Hendessi, M (1996)
Survey of Young Carers in Hammersmith and Fulham Caring for Carers Association.
Produced by Linx Research and Training Consultancy.

Tabulates young carers by age, ethnicity and the relatives they look after.

Hertfordshire County Council, Youth And Community Service (1997)
Hertfordshire Youth and Community Service 1996–97.
Hertfordshire Youth and Community Service.

Annual report describing the work of Hertfordshire Youth and Community Service. It includes projects and work around youth information, environmental education, youth councils, crime prevention, motor projects, work with young carers, rural youth work, arts, voluntary sector work, and training. It also includes a questionnaire for comments on the future work of the service.

Heron, C. (1998)
Working with Carers.
London: Jessica Kingsley Publishers.

Achieves a balance between day-to-day practicalities (including chapters on young carers, parents of children with disabilities and of people with mental health problems) and wider social issues.

Howard, M. (2001)
Paying the Price: Carers, poverty and social exclusion.
Carers UK.

Keith, L. and Morris, J. (1995)
'Easy targets: a disability rights perspective on the "children as carers" debate', in *Critical Social Policy*, 44/45: 36–57.

Landells, S. and Pritlove, I. (1994)
Young Carers of a Parent with Schizophrenia: A Leeds survey.
Leeds: Department of Social Services.

A survey of mental health and child care professionals in contact with children caring for parents with schizophrenia.

Lowestoft Primary Care Trust (2001)
Identifying Young Carers and Meeting their Needs: Final report.
Lowestoft Primary Care Trust.

Findings of a multi-agency, multi-disciplinary research programme seeking to identify the needs of young carers and consider how existing practice could be developed to support them.

Lupton, C. (ed) (2000)
Moving Forward on Family Group Conferences in Hampshire.
University of Portsmouth.

Madge, N., et al. (2000)
9 to 13: The forgotten years?
London: National Children's Bureau.

A wide-ranging review of the key issues affecting this age group as they pass into puberty, change schools and become more independent from the family. The numbers in difficulty, including young carers, runaways, looked after children, school exclusions, suicide, drugs and smoking. The authors conclude that the evidence strongly supports the case for more attention to be paid to the needs and difficulties of pre-adolescent children.

McClure, L. (2001)
'School-Age Caregivers: Perceptions of school nurses working in Central England' in *The Journal of School Nursing*, Vol. 17, No. 2 pp. 76–82.

McNeish, D. and Johnson, E. (1997)
Report on a joint evaluation of Bradford Young Carers and the Willow Scheme [in Leeds]
Barnardo's Yorkshire Division.

Mahon, A. and Higgins, I. (1995)
'...A Life of our Own' Young Carers: An evaluation of three RHA-funded projects in Merseyside.
University of Manchester: Health Services Management Unit.

This is an evaluation of the young carers' projects in Sefton, St Helens and Knowsley, and provides information about the organisation and management of the projects, and demographic information about the localities in which they are based. Interviews and quotes from both young carers and their parent(s) about the effects of caring are included. The report also contains a discussion of interviews with senior managers.

Metcalfe, J. (2000)
Signpost Stockport Young Carers' Conference April 2000 Report.
Stockport: Signpost Stockport (Torkington Centre, Torkington Road, Hazel Grove, Stockport SK7 4PY).

Key findings from a conference aimed at providing a platform for discussion of the main issues facing young carers, and an opportunity to consult directly with young people regarding the effectiveness of existing services and service development. The conference workshops also aimed to help young carers build on their skills and empower them for decision-making.

Munoz, N. (1998)
Young Carers and their Families in Westminster.
Westminster Carers Service.

Findings of a project aimed at identifying the population of young carers in Westminster and providing an account of their responsibilities and needs. Explores ways of accessing resources and makes recommendations for future inter-agency arrangements for assessment and service provision.

Newton, B. and Becker, S. (1996)
Young Carers in Southwark: The hidden face of community care.
Loughborough University: Young Carers Research Group.

This research report provides an in-depth analysis of the experiences of a dozen young carers in the London Borough of Southwark. The findings and conclusions led to the implementation of Capital Carers, a young carers' project.

Nixon, P. (1999)
'Promoting Family Decision-making in Child Care Practice' in *Child Care in Practice: Northern Ireland Journal of Multi-Disciplinary Child Care Practice*, Volume 5 No 4 pp. 308–327

Olsen, R. (1996)
'Young carers: challenging the facts and politics of research into children and caring' in *Disability and Society*, 11: 1: 41–54.

Olsen, R. (2000)
'Families under the Microscope: Parallels between the young carers debate of the 1990s and the transformation of childhood in the late nineteenth century' in *Children and Society* Vol. 14 pp. 384–394.

Olsen, R. and Parker, G. (1997)
'A response to Aldridge and Becker – "Disability rights and the denial of young carers: the dangers of zero-sum arguments"' in *Critical Social Policy*, 50: 125–33.

Parker, G. and Olsen, R. (1995)
A Sideways Glance at Young Carers.
Nuffield Community Care Studies Unit, University of Leicester.

Looks at the available statistics relating to young carers.

Salter, June (1999)
The Health Needs of Young Carers: A pilot study.
London: The Children's Society.

Seddon, D. et al. (2001)
A Study of Young Carers in Wales: Report to the Wales Office of Research and Development for Health and Social Care.
Centre for Social Policy Research & Development, Institute of Medical and Social Care Research, University of Wales, Bangor.

Tatum, C. et al.
Northern Ireland Young Carers: An exploration of their needs and of the response by Crossroads Caring for Carers (NI) Ltd
Open University

Thomas, N. (2001)
A Study of Young Carers in Wales: Perspectives of children and young people.
Centre for Applied Social Studies, University of Wales, Swansea.

Violence Against Children Study Group (1999)
Children, Child Abuse and Child Protection: Placing children centrally.
Chichester: Wiley

Collection of contributions from a multi-disciplinary group of researchers and practitioners. Topics covered include: Black children and the child protection system; young carers; children and adolescents who abuse; domestic violence; decision-making in case conferences; schools and child protection; primary prevention and the role of the health visitor; child protection in relation to the current emphasis on core policing; children in residential care; preventing institutional abuse.

Walker, A. (1996)
Young Carers and their Families: A survey carried out by the Social Survey Division of the Office for National Statistics on behalf of the Department of Health.
London: The Stationery Office.

A report of the first government survey of young carers. Includes information from young carers and professionals and attempts to extrapolate figures for the number of young carers nationally. The official estimate is between 19,000 and 51,000.

York Council (1999)
Working with Carers – The Next Decade: A joint strategy for North Yorkshire and York.

Other resources on young carers for professionals

Carers in Hertfordshire (1997)
Make Sure They're Alright.

A peer-led video and information pack about what it is like to take care of somebody.

Carers National Association (1997)
Young Carers' Information Pack.

The Children's Society (2000)
Young Carers and Our Families – Video

A video of young carers talking about their lives and giving messages for practitioners.

Cornwall Young Carers Project (2001)
Who Cares?

Video

Hammersmith and Fulham Young Carers
What about me?

This video was put together by young people who have a caring role in their family and expresses their views about being young carers.

NCH Action for Children (1997)
Factfile '98.

Includes a section on young carers.

NCH Action for Children
Carefree – Young Carers Video

Examines young carers' emotions and responsibilities by using four short stories. Video work pack and board game, available in English or Welsh.

Available from NCH Action for Children, Ty Eluned, Towyn Road, Abergele, LL22 9AA

Taylor, A. (1999)
Developing a Befriending Scheme: A toolkit for practitioners.
London: The Children's Society.

UK Youth (2001)
Perspectives on Young Carers.

Wakefield District Young Carers
Information Pack.

A learning resource to be used with groups of children and young people. It is designed to raise awareness of young carers and is useful for schools. It looks at how to identify young carers, provides information about young carer schemes and examines issues such as confidentiality and coping with stress.

Legislation and guidance

Brunt, S. (1999)
Improving Children's Health: A survey of 1999–2000 Health Improvement Programmes.
London: NSPCC.

Department for Education and Employment (1999a)
National Healthy Schools Standard: Guidance.
Available to download free of charge at: www.dfes.gov.uk

Department for Education and Employment (1999b)
School Inclusion: Pupil Support (Circular No 10/99).

The Secretary of State's guidance on pupil attendance, behaviour, exclusion and re-integration. Available from Department for Education and Employment (tel. 0845 7602 2260); website: www.dfes.gov.uk

Department of Health (1996a)
Young Carers: Something to Think About. Report of four SSI workshops May–July 1995.
London: Department of Health.

The workshops referred to in the title were part of the Department of Health's programme of work on young carers. The report draws on these workshops to suggest means of identifying young carers; supporting them using a whole-family approach; and a multi-agency approach to meeting needs. The papers presented at the workshops are also available separately from the Department of Health.

Department of Health (1996b)
Young Carers – Making a Start: Report of the SSI fieldwork project on families with disability or illness, October 1995–January 1996.
London: Department of Health.

An official report of the Department of Health's three-year programme of work on young carers. Primarily intended for, and written about, social services departments. The report includes case studies, examples of good practice and a review of local authorities' policies on young carers.

Department of Health (1996c)
Carers (Recognition and Services) Act 1995: Policy guidance and practice guide.
London: Department of Health.

Department of Health, Department for Education and Employment, Home Office (2000)
Framework for the Assessment of Children in Need and their Families.
London: The Stationery Office.

Department of Health (1999a)
Working Together to Safeguard Children: A guide to inter-agency working to safeguard and promote the welfare of children.
Quality Protects, Department of Health.

Department of Health (1999b)
National Framework for Mental Health (1999).
Available from: www.doh.gov.uk/nsf/mentalhealth

Standard 6 is relevant to work with young carers and their families.

Department of Health (1999c)
Caring about Carers: A National Strategy for Carers.
Available from: www.doh.gov.uk

Department of Health (2000)
A Jigsaw of Services: Inspection of services to support disabled adults in their parenting role. Key messages for practitioners and first-line managers.
Available from Department of Health Publications, PO Box 777, London SE1 6XH

Department of Health
NHS and Community Care Act 1990 Guidance.
Available from Department of Health Publications (see above)

Department of Health (2001)
The Carers and Disabled Children Act 2000 Guidance.
Available from Department of Health Publications (see above)

Department of Health
NHS Priorities Guidance 1999.
Available from: www.doh.gov.uk/nsf/mentalhealth

Department of Health (2002)
Fair Access to Care Services: Guidance on eligibility criteria for adult social care.
Available free to download from: www.doh.gov.uk

Acts of Parliament

All Acts of Parliament from 1998 onwards are available, free to download from the Stationary Office website: www.hmso.gov.uk

Alcohol and drug dependency

Books for professionals

Alcohol Concern (1997)
Measures for Measures: A framework for alcohol policy.

Brisby, T. (1997)
Under the Influence: Coping with parents who drink too much.
Alcohol Concern

Childline (1997)
Beyond the Limit: Children who live with parental alcohol misuse.

A report describing what children themselves have to say about parental drinking, based on calls coming in to Childline.

Cleaver, H., Unell, I. and Aldgate, J. (1999)
Children's Needs – Parenting Capacity: The impact of parental mental illness, problem alcohol and drug use, and domestic violence on children's development.
London: The Stationery Office.

An exploration of the research literature shows that these potential problems affect children differently depending on their age and individual circumstances.

Harbin, F. and Murphy, M. (eds) (2000)
Substance Misuse and Childcare: How to understand, assist and intervene when drugs affect parenting.
Russell House Publishing.

Hogg, C., Chadwick, T. and Dale-Perera, A. (1997)
Drug-using Parents: Policy guidelines for inter-agency working.
London: Local Government Association.

Laybourn, A., Brown, J., Hill, M. (1996)
Hurting on the Inside: Children's experiences of parental alcohol misuse.
Aldershot: Avebury.

Lifeline Manchester
Telling the Truth about Drugs.

Publications catalogue re: alcohol and drugs.
Tel. 0161 839 2054

Liverpool Health and Alcohol Team (2001)
In a Different World: Parental drug and alcohol use – a consultation into its effects on children and families in Liverpool.

Tunnard, J. (2002)
Parental Drug Misuse: A review of impact and intervention.
Research In Practice

Books and resources on alcohol and drug dependency suitable for young people

Al-Anon Family Groups
A range of pamphlets for young people who have a family member who suffers from alcoholism:
Courage to be Me
If your parents drink too much
Hope for Children of Alcoholics: Alateen
What's 'Drunk', Mummy?

Brooks, C.
The Secret Everyone Knows.

Help for young people for whom alcohol is a problem in their home.

Brow, C., LaPorte, B. and Moe, J.
Kids Power Too – words to grow by.

Hastings, J. and Typpo, M.
An Elephant in the Living Room.

Jones, P.
The Brown Bottle.

Two books for young people who have a family member who is an alcoholic.

Lifeline Manchester
Young Carers.

Leaflet aimed at young people caring for someone within the family who has a problem with drugs or alcohol.
Tel: 0161 8392054

Lifeline Manchester
The Big Blue Book of Booze.

Information for younger people. Gives information/facts on what alcohol is and does to you. Content should be viewed first.

Leite, E. and Espeland, P.
Different Like Me.

A book for teens who worry about their parents' use of alcohol or drugs.

SCAD (Support for Children Affected by Drink)
Worried about your parents' drinking? and
Concerned about someone's drinking?

Two leaflets about the effects of parents' drinking on children, with notes giving information about alcohol and how to get help.
Tel: 01905 230600

Scottish Council on Alcohol.
Is someone drinking too much where you live?

Audio cassette for children about what happens when someone is drinking too much.

Scottish Council on Alcohol (1994)
Drinkwise Scotland.

Factsheets and audio tape for children of problem drinkers.

Bereavement

For professionals

Holland, J. (2001)
Understanding Children's Experiences of Parental Bereavement.
London: Jessica Kingsley Publishers.

Holland, J.
Coping with Bereavement: A handbook for teachers.
Cardiff Academic Press.

Books and resources on bereavement for use with young people

Cruse – Bereavement Care
My Father Died; My Mother Died;
Caring for Bereaved Children.

Booklets for children.
Tel: 020 8940 4818

LeBlanc, S. (1998)
A Dragon in Your Heart.
London: Jessica Kingsley Publishers

Book aimed at explaining cancer to young children.

Nystrom C.
Emma Says Goodbye.

Sensitive account of an aunt's terminal care at home.

Black communities and other cultures

Barn, R. (2001)
Black Youth on the Margins: A research review
York: Joseph Rowntree Foundation.

Dwivedi, K. N. (2002)
Meeting the Needs of Ethnic Minority Children – Including Refugee, Black and Mixed Parentage Children: A handbook for professionals.
London: Jessica Kingsley Publishers.

Gavin, J. (1991)
I want to be an Angel.
London: Mammoth.

A collection of children's stories; including one about a Black young carer.

Greater Manchester Black Young Carers Workshop Working Group (1996)
Working with Black Young Carers: A framework for change.
Manchester: The Greater Manchester Black Young Carers' Working Group.

This report discusses how and why Black young carers have previously been overlooked and suggests how service providers and practitioners can examine their own procedures to ensure that the needs of Black young carers are identified and met. Also contains useful references and further reading.

Hussain, Y., Atkin, K. and Ahmad, W. (2002)
South Asian Disabled Young People and their Families.
York: Joseph Rowntree Foundation, Policy Press.

Jones, A., Jeyasingham, D. and Rajasooriya, S. (2002)
Invisible Families: The strengths and needs of Black families in which young people have caring responsibilities.
York: Joseph Rowntree Foundation.
www.jrf.org.uk

Karmi, G. (1996)
The Ethnic Health Handbook: A factfile for health care professionals.
Oxford: Blackwell Science.

King's Fund Centre (1992)
Young Carers in Black and Minority Ethnic Communities: Workshop day report.
London: King's Fund Centre.

This report, based on a one-day conference at the King's Fund Centre, examines the issues surrounding Black and minority ethnic young carers. It is one of the few reports available of this kind.

Powell, E. et al. (2002)
We Care Too: A good practice guide for people working with Black carers.
National Black Carers Workers Network in association with The Afiya Trust.

Shah, R., and Hatton, C. (1999)
Caring Alone: Young carers in South Asian Communities.
Ilford: Barnardo's.

Research focusing on the experiences of young carers who were in contact with two Barnardo's young carers' projects. Major themes identified included: the kinds of tasks and roles performed; the contexts in which caring was carried out; and the consequences, provision of support services.

Vernon, A. (2002)
User-defined Outcomes of Community Care for Asian Disabled People.
York: Joseph Rowntree Foundation, Policy Press.

Disability/illness

Books for professionals

The Association of Disabled Parents in the Norfolk Area [PANDA]
Families First Survey detailing the findings of disabled parents of school-aged children.
Tel. 01553 768193.

Fieldhouse, R. (ed.) (2001)
AIDS Reference Manual.
NAM Publications.

Grimshaw, R. (1991)
Children of Parents with Parkinson's Disease: A research report for the Parkinson's Disease Society.
London: National Children's Bureau.

This piece of research looks at the effects of Parkinson's Disease on children in families, and covers areas such as the medical knowledge children possess, their home life and how their parents' illness affects them.

Imrie, J. and Coombes, Y. (1995)
No Time to Waste: The scale and dimensions of the problem of children affected by HIV/AIDS in localities in the United Kingdom.
Ilford: Bamardo's.

A report on children affected, rather than infected, by HIV/AIDS in the family. The report seeks to establish current figures and project future ones for the number of children, families and communities affected; and discusses responses that reflect children's needs and service provision.

Lewis, E. (2001a)
Afraid to Say: The needs and views of young people living with HIV/AIDS.
London: National Children's Bureau.

Findings of a study aiming to place children's voices at the centre of the debate about service provision for young people and children living with HIV/AIDS.

Lewis, E (2001b)
Children and young people living with HIV/AIDS.
London: National Children's Bureau.

Marcenko, M.O. and Samost, L.
Living with HIV/AIDS: The voices of HIV positive mothers.

Murray, P. and Penman, J. (Eds) (2000)
Telling Our Own Stories: Reflections on family life in a disabling world.
Parents with Attitude.

National AIDS Trust (1998)
Families and AIDS: A review of support services for HIV-affected families and carers in the UK.

Summarises some of the fundamental issues surrounding HIV/AIDS-affected families and recommends areas for development.

Segal, J. and Simkins, J. (1993)
My Mum Needs Me: Helping children with ill or disabled parents.
London: Penguin.

This book examines the experiences of children with sick or disabled parents. Most of the children concerned have a parent with multiple sclerosis and some perform a caring role. Included are many quotes from both parents and children who have undergone counselling.

Segal, J. and Simkins, J. (1996)
Helping Children with Ill or Disabled Parents: A guide for parents and professionals.
London: Jessica Kingsley.

An updated version of *My Mum Needs Me* which incorporates a chapter aimed at professionals who either work with clients with illnesses or disabilities or who work directly with the children of ill or disabled parents.

Stroke Association
Younger People have Strokes Too.

A survey of the experiences of younger people affected by stroke.
Tel: 020 7490 7999

Wates, M. (2002)
Supporting Disabled Adults in their Parenting Role.
York: Joseph Rowntree Foundation.

Books and resources on disability and illness for use with young people

Arthritis Care
A Day with Sam.

Booklet aimed at younger children about a little girl who has arthritis.
Tel: 020 7916 1500

The British Epilepsy Association
My Mum Has Epilepsy.

Typed document aimed at young children (includes drawings).

The British Epilepsy Association
New Horizons.

A guide for young people with epilepsy. General information aimed at older children.

Laird, E. (2001)
Red Sky in the Morning.
Basingstoke: Macmillan Children's Books.

Fiction for children about a young girl who has a disabled brother.

The Medicine Group (UK) Ltd
Learning about Epilepsy.

Illustrated simple textbook especially for younger children.
Publishing House, 62 Stert Street, Abingdon, Oxon., OX14 3UQ

Motor Neurone Association
When your Parent has Motor Neurone Disease.

Booklet aimed at young people with information on caring and feelings.
Tel: 01604 250505

Multiple Sclerosis Society
Has your Mum or Dad got MS?

Booklet aimed at young people. Information on what MS is and child's feelings.
Tel: 020 7610 7171

Multiple Sclerosis Society
My Mum's got MS.

Booklet in story format, aimed at young children explaining what MS is like.
Tel: 020 7610 7171

Roby Education Ltd
The Illustrated Junior Encyclopaedia of Epilepsy.

Information written in A–Z format about epilepsy.
Roby Education Ltd., 3 Lyndhurst, Maghull, Merseyside, L31 6DY

Saunders, K. (2000)
Happy Ever Afters – a storybook guide to teaching children about disability.
Trentham Books.

Education

Marsden, R. (1995)
Young Carers and Education.
London: Borough of Enfield, Education Department.

This report describes the results of a survey of schools and statutory and voluntary agencies in Enfield. The results demonstrate that the majority of young carers identified experienced educational difficulties, the most common ones being problems with punctuality; poor attendance; and problems with homework/coursework. The report contains brief case studies and summaries of interviews with professionals.

Mental Health Foundation (2002)
Peer Support Manual: A guide to setting up a peer listening project in education settings.
Mental Health Foundation.

Guide as to how schools can go about setting up a peer listening service, complete with case studies, handouts and training material. Would be useful for: teachers, school counsellors, youth workers, policy makers and voluntary sector organisations.

Other resources for schools

Baker, G.
Supporting Young Carers in School: A secondary resource pack.
Carers Lewisham, Princess Royal Trust for Carers.

Includes lesson plan ideas and resources.

Baker, K., Sillett, J. with Neary, S. (2000)
Citizenship: Challenges for Councils.
The Education Network and the Local Government Information Unit.

Contains useful addresses, names of organisations and websites.

Carers Together in Hampshire (2001)
Who Cares? Young Carers PSHE Pack: Pupil awareness module for use in schools.

Includes case studies and worksheets for use in lessons.

Northamptonshire Young Carers' Service (2001)
Information Pack for Schools.

Folder of information, including lesson ideas.

Suffolk County Council (2001)
Understanding Young Carers: A support document for PSE (Key Stage 3, Year 8).

Includes background information and resources for lessons.

Surrey Young Carers' Project (1998)
Young Carers: Resource Pack for Schools.

Includes photocopiable resources and information.

(See also resources listed under 'Young Carers' above.)

Mental health

Department of Health (1998)
Crossing Bridges – Training Support Programme: Parental mental illness and its implications for children.
Brighton: Pavilion Publishing Ltd.

Depression Alliance
Caring for Carers.

Booklet with information on caring for someone with depression.
Tel. 020 7721 7672

Dutt, R. and Ferns, P. (1998)
Letting Through Light: A training pack on black people and mental health.
London: REU.

Falkov, A. (1997)
Parental Psychiatric Disorder and Child Maltreatment, Part II: Extent and nature of the association.
London: National Children's Bureau.

Briefing which explores the association between psychiatric conditions affecting parents and child maltreatment. It looks at the influence of maternal depression on parenting and related topics such as family violence, parental self-harm and young carers. It also discusses possible opportunities for intervention.

Health Education Authority
Survival Diary.

One-year diary 1997/98 for young people, looking at feelings, with advice and information.
Tel: 020 7222 5300

Keeping Children In Mind Conference (1998)
Keeping Children in Mind: Balancing children's needs with parents' mental health.
Michael Sieff Foundation.

Report of the 12th annual conference hosted by the Michael Sieff Foundation, held at Cumberland Lodge, September 1997. Short papers on a wide range of topics, including child protection, parents with learning disabilities, young carers, various organisational viewpoints, and an address by Paul Boateng, MP.

National Schizophrenia Fellowship
Schizophrenia Leaflet.
www.nsf.org.uk

Information on schizophrenia.

Wright, S. and Bell, M. (2000)
The 'Us Too' Group: A psychodynamic perspective on the impact of parental mental ill health on young carers.
Gloucestershire Young Carers' Project.

Other resources on mental health for professionals

Department of Health (2001)
Contact: A directory of mental health.
Available from: www.doh.gov.uk

A directory of useful contacts and organisations for working in the field of mental health.

Eating Disorders Association (2002)
It's not about food, it's about feelings.
www.edauk.com

An educational resource.

Gray, G.
Talking About It: Promoting mental health in schools.
Meridian Broadcasting Charitable Trust.

A pack for use in schools with 11–16-year-olds.
Tel: 02380 236806

Books and other resources on mental health for use with young people

Alzheimer's Disease Society
It's enough to blow your mind – Alzheimer's.

Basic leaflet about Alzheimer's for children.
Tel: 020 7306 0606

Crossroads 'Caring for Carers'
Do you know someone who is going to hospital?

Leaflet detailing some questions that children may ask if a family member with a mental health problem is going into hospital.

Liverpool Joint Consultative Committee (1999)
Young Carers' Mental Health Resource Pack: Making young carers count in Liverpool.

A resource pack about mental health for young carers. Contains cartoons which explain mental health to children and young people.

Manic Depression Fellowship
Why did my world have to change?

Leaflet for teenagers whose parents have manic depression.
Tel: 020 8974 6550

MIND
How to Survive Family Life and
How to recognise the early signs of mental distress

Short booklets for older children on family life/mental health issues.
Tel: 020 8519 2122

Signpost Young Carers Project
What is mental illness?

Information pack to help young people understand more about the difference between mental health and mental illness.

Young Minds

Young Minds produces a number of booklets for young people. One of the booklets is called 'Mental illness in your family' and is written with young carers in mind. See www.youngminds.org.uk for further information.

Participation

'Giving Young People a Say' in *Rural Focus* 1995/96 Winter Issue (no. 8)

In many villages, teenagers have little control over their lives. Activities and facilities, where they exist at all, are planned for them. Transport means walking or begging parents for a lift. Little wonder that so many rural young people feel frustration and a sense of alienation. Several counties are experimenting with youth parish councils to give young people a more active role in the local community.

'How to Involve Young People in Decision-making' in *Red Cross Education*, Summer 2000 issue, pp. 10–11.

There is a boom in practical attempts to involve young people in decision-making. This short article advises on the approach to take when setting up youth councils, youth forums, young people's committees, etc. and where you can get further information.

Badham B. (2001)
'Count us in', *Childright*, issue no. 174, pp. 14–17.

Examines recent initiatives such as the government's national strategy for neighbourhood renewal, local strategic partnerships and the Children's Fund; and discusses ways of effectively involving children and young people in consultation and decision-making.

Benga, A. et al. (2001)
The Emperor's New Clothes: A report on three conferences exploring children's rights.
London: National Children's Bureau.

Written by the young people themselves, this publication highlights the lessons that have been learned from the experiences of a group of young people who organised a series of conferences around participation. Through commissioning the conferences on involvement in decision-making, the children and young people illustrated just how much can be accomplished through participation.

Booth T. et al. (2000)
Index for Inclusion: Developing learning and participation in schools.
Centre for Studies on Inclusive Education.

A set of materials to support schools in a process of inclusive school development by drawing on the views of staff, governors, parents and students. Sets out a step-by-step process of change and examines ways in which inclusive practices can be developed by incorporating the values and cultures held within the school and community. The dimensions of culture, policy and practice are used to direct thinking about school change and to bring about inclusion within the educational process. Barriers to learning and participation are examined.

Cash K. (2000)
'Target: youth participation and skills development' in *Images* 6(1) pp. 4–6.

Article on Y Care's Target campaign, which aims to raise awareness of the importance of addressing young peoples' skills needs.

Clarkson J. and Frank J. (2000)
'The Voice of the Child in FGCs' in *Moving Forward on Family Group Conferences in Hampshire: Development and research.*

Describes the work undertaken by The Children's Society's Rights and Participation Team in Hampshire to evaluate the extent to which the voice of the child is heard in family group conferences.

Dickenson, B. (2000)
The Youth of Today have Something to Say… about Participation: The story of the Participation Education Group – a registered charity run by and for young people.
Participation Education Group.

PEG members have explained their thinking about what makes participation work, and the book includes extracts from pieces of research that PEG has carried out, including the evaluation of their scheme for peer education for participation.

Kalra V.S., Fieldhouse E.A. and Alam, S. (2001)
'Avoiding the New Deal: A case study of non-participation by minority ethnic young people' in *Youth and Policy*, Summer 2001 issue, no.72.

Kinney, L. and McCabe J. (2001)
Children as Partners: A guide to consulting with very young children and empowering them to participate effectively.
Stirling Council.

The rights of children to be consulted and listened to on matters affecting them are enshrined in legislation. Ensuring that children's voices are heard and their involvement in decision-making encouraged can be a challenge for early years practitioners and service providers. This guide is offered as a support for staff in nurseries and early years establishments.

Miller, J. (1996)
Never Too Young: How young children can take responsibility and make decisions – a handbook for early years workers.
National Early Years Network.

This practical handbook shows how young children, under the age of eight, can participate, make decisions and take responsibility for their actions.

Rights and Participation Hampshire (2000)
The Needs of Young Carers and our Families: A report on the participation of young carers at 'community care live – 2000'.
London: The Children's Society.

Rotherham Participation Project (2001)
Young People's Charter of Participation.
London: The Children's Society.

Rotherham Participation Project, together with young people in Rotherham, developed the Charter using research involving over 400 young people. The research looked at specific subjects of concern for young people, including health, housing, crime, education, training and employment. Young people's views enabled the project to identify the common themes that were creating barriers to young people accessing services or being involved in decision-making.

Willow, C. (2001)
Participation in Practice: Children and young people as partners in change.
London: The Children's Society.

Includes a chapter on the work done at the annual Young Carers' Festivals in partnership with YMCA Fairthorne Manor.

Refugees and asylum-seekers

Colin-Thorne, D. (2002)
Meeting the Health Needs of Refugee and Asylum-Seekers in the UK: An information and resource pack for health workers.
Available (with updates) from the Department of Health website (www.doh.gov.uk)

Panter-Brick, C. and Smith, M.T. (eds) (2000)
Abandoned Children.
Cambridge University Press.

Book about issues surrounding refugee children.

Refugee Children's Consortium (2002)
Response by the Refugee Children's Consortium to the Home Office White Paper 'Secure Borders, Safe Haven: Integration with Diversity in Modern Britain'.

Refugee Council (March 2002)
The Refugee Council's Response to the Government's White Paper 'Secure Borders, Safe Haven: Integration with Diversity in Modern Britain'.
Refugee Council.

Refugee Council (2002)
Briefing July 2002: Health services for asylum-seekers and refugees.
Available from the Refugee Council website: www.refugeecouncil.org.uk

Roberts, K. and Harris, J. (2002)
Disabled People in Refugee and Asylum-Seeking Communities.
Policy Press for Joseph Rowntree Foundation.

Tolfree, D. (1996)
Restoring Playfulness: Different approaches to assisting children who are psychologically affected by war or displacement.
Falun: Scandbook.

The Department of Health has issued an information and resource pack for refugees and asylum-seekers which includes a section on eligibility for and provision of health services.
www.london.nhs/newsmedia/publications.htm

Siblings

Atkinson, N. and Crawforth, M. (1995)
All in the Family: Siblings and disability.
London: NCH Action for Children.

A survey of children with disabled siblings – the report suggests that all of the children have great affection for their siblings but that they experience some problems in terms of social isolation, problems at school and public attitudes to disability. All of the children in the survey were involved in some aspects of caring for their disabled sibling.

British Institute of Learning Disabilities [BILD]
Brothers, Sisters and Learning Disability.

Booklet giving information for families who have a child with learning disabilities, and other children in the family.
Tel: 01562 850251

Cairo, S. (1999)
Our Brother Has Down's Syndrome: An introduction for children.
Annick Press Ltd.

Book explaining Down's Syndrome to young siblings and young children.

Contact a Family.
Siblings and Special Needs.

Factsheet about siblings of children with a severe disability/chronic illness. For parents and those working with families who have a child with special needs.

Mental Health Foundation
Children with Autism.

Booklet for siblings of someone with autism.

National Autistic Society.
Siblings of Children with Autism.

Guide to understanding sibling relationships, what families can do to support their other children. National Autistic Society, 276 Willesden Lane, London, NW2 5RB

NCH Action for Children.
Hello Sister! Hello Brother! All in the Family.

Leaflet giving advice for both young people/parents who have a brother or sister/child with a disability.

Youth work

Factor, F., Chauhan, V. and Pitts, J. (eds) (2001)
The RHP Companion to Working with Young People.
Russell House Publishing.

Ingram, G. and Harris, J. (2001)
Delivering Good Youth Work: A working guide to surviving and thriving.
Russell House Publishing.

Plummer, D. (2001)
Helping Children to Build Self-Esteem.
London: Jessica Kingsley Publishers.

A photocopiable activities book.

Rogers, V. (2001)
Exploring Feelings: A resource handbook for work with young people aged 9 to 13.
Youth Work Press.